OCCULT DATA

Copyright, 1921
by
ELBERT BENJAMINE

Serial No. 39

THE CHURCH OF LIGHT
Box 1525, Los Angeles 53, California

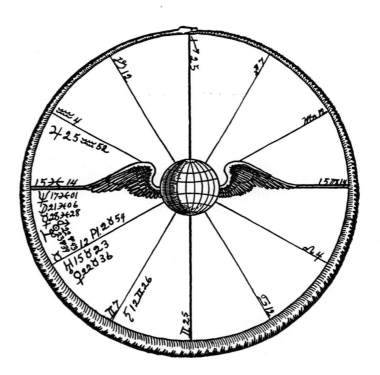

Birth-chart of T. H. Burgoyne, Apr. 14, 1855, 4:11 a.m. 3 W. 54 N.
Great seer (Moon, Mercury and Neptune on Asc.) and daring
pioneer (Sun conjunction Mars in Aries) in placing The Brotherhood of Light teachings before the world. Light of Egypt, Vol. 1,
published in 1889, was responsible for Elbert Benjamine, who under
his pen name, C. C. Zain, later wrote all 210 Brotherhood of Light
lessons, making a thorough study of astrology. This book and Art
Magic, and Ghostland, by another author, all three now out of print,
were the outstanding expositions of Brotherhood of Light teachings
until the more detailed Brotherhood of Light lessons were issued.

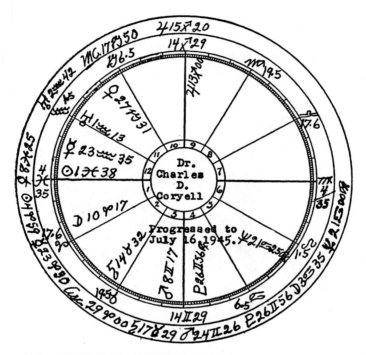

DR. CHARLES D. CORYELL, February 21, 1912, 6:45 a.m.
PST. 118:15W. 34N. Data given by a relative.

1940, started teaching at University of California at Los Angeles:
Mercury trine Jupiter *p* in house of teaching (ninth).

1942, May, asked to go to San Francisco for conference on research leading to manufacture of atomic bomb: Sun at birth in house
of secret things (twelfth), sextile Uranus *r*, planet of invention and
research.

1945, July 16, with other parents of the atomic bomb, was present
at Aloma, New Mexico, when first atomic bomb was dropped: First
atomic bomb used in warfare was dropped on Hiroshima, Aug. 6,
1945, hastening end of World War II: Jupiter conjunction M.C. *r;*
Mars trine Mercury *r;* Mercury sextile Mercury *r;* sextile Mars *p;*
semi-square Venus *p;* semi-square Mars *r.*

OCCULT DATA

THE WORD occult means that which is hidden. Occultism, consequently, is the science of hidden forces, and the art of subjecting such forces to human control. Here we will consider the data upon which occultism rests.

Its subjects are not directly apprehended by the five senses upon which the physical scientist relies for all knowledge. The line of demarcation between that which is called occult is, therefore, constantly changing; for scientists every now and then invent a device by which some hitherto occult force is made directly perceptible to the physical senses. It is then no longer considered occult.

Not long since, for instance, the power of the lodestone was held to be occult. Indeed, so far as any knowledge of its nature is concerned, the physical scientists should include the force of gravitation in the occult category; for they admit it operates across immense space in which there is nothing that can be apprehended by the five senses, yet fail to explain by what hidden means the force is transmitted.

The infra-red and ultra-violet rays of light, also were occult a few years ago, and are so yet to the majority of people.

All mental forces fall properly into this category, as is admitted in the case of hypnotism, exhibiting, as it does, the power of one mind over another.

It is clear, then, that the common application of the word occult, since it depends upon the experience of the speaker—for what is hidden to one may be perceived by another—is wholly arbitrary.

Man Fears That Which He Does Not Understand. —The word carries with it an air of mystery, it is true; but all forces are mysterious to those who have not studied them; and what is mysterious to the ignorant is obvious to the learned. Yet in all nature, nothing can come permanently under this ban; for all mysteries may be solved. Thus the simplest conveniences of modern civilization are mysterious to the untutored savage. He is wont to attribute their power to some supernatural agency. But there is nothing supernatural—nothing, that is, not governed by natural laws. Above and below, all obey those by which they manifest; and while these laws are uncomprehended any phenomenon seems mysterious.

It was this uncomprehension that caused the terror of the Red Man, who, not understanding the natural laws underlying its geysers and boiling paint-pots, feared to enter the Yellowstone Park; while the White Man, sure that its riddles could be solved, has made it his national playground. And just as the savage inclines to attribute such phenomena to some supernatural agency, or similarly to attribute the powers of the burning-glass, and to regard photographs with reverence, so other men, more highly endowed, but not less ignorant in that special direction, can see in spiritual phenomena only Divine intervention and miracles.

Thus do all of us fear that which we do not understand; but with understanding comes courage, for with the dawning of the light of the mind we see how any hidden danger—if danger there be—may be circumvented. Knowledge reveals it either as a scare-crow or as a menace, the one to be ignored and the other avoided except as it can be made subservient to the will of man.

Progression Depends Upon Knowledge.—Man's only progression, here or hereafter, must be founded on knowledge. Only by its means can he subjugate his external environment and enjoy its opportunities. He who is ignorant of the laws of his physical body incurs illness. He who is ignorant of the laws governing acquisition remains in poverty. He who is ignorant of the social laws of his land is likely to be deprived of his liberty.

So it is also with things spiritual. Only through a knowledge of spiritual laws can man mold his spiritual environment and enjoy, while yet on earth, spiritual powers. Ignorant of the laws of his spiritual body, he incurs moral maladies that follow him beyond the tomb. Ignorant of the laws governing the acquisition of spiritual attributes, he misses the greatest treasures of this life, and passes to the life beyond in spiritual poverty. If, still ignorant, he goes to the new life with no knowledge of the laws and customs of the denizens of that realm, or if he contacts them while he is still embodied, he may, in his unenlightened condition, be deprived of his liberty. Only through knowledge of himself, and of the powers and forces by which he is environed, can he expect to progress. And it is for this reason that the occultist applies himself to the acquisition of such knowledge.

Its acquisition, like everything else, depends much upon a proper beginning, and the occult student, starting out on his voyage in search of the Golden Fleece of spiritual truth, needs to take care that he sets sail from the right port and in the right direction. At the very beginning, then, of our bold enterprise, in which we purpose to carry the student safely across the muddy tide of metaphysics and land him securely on the bright shores of occult knowledge, we must indicate our port of debarkation and show it to be a true port.

All Knowledge Is Based Upon Experience.—No better starting point can be found for such a purpose, nor another nearly so strong and well defended, as the fundamental assertion, I AM.

Following Nature as our safest pilot, we discover that the first glimmer of consciousness—that which foreshadows knowledge—is concerned with distinguishing the Me from the Not-me. Thus a sensation registers as something distinct from me but affecting me; and it matters not whether we accept the statement of the Cartesian school, "I think, therefore I am," or prefer the version of Eliphas Levi, the learned French Magus, "I am, therefore I think," the fact remains that the assertion "I AM" is irrefutable.

By no quirk of speculation can we deny the existence of the thinker, who must postulate a being able to think before he can find ground on which to stand to make denial. When he admits the existence of a being able to form an opinion, he has established himself as an entity; for, clearly, if there is no thinker, there can be no thought; and if there is no thought there can be no denial. Consequently, no one can deny his own existence; and from this undeniable premise any correct system of philosophy must start.

The consciousness of the thinker, thus firmly established, is a perception of relations. These relations may be subjective or objective, but to be conscious of them he must be able to compare them. Where there is no change, no relative conditions, there can be no consciousness.

Similarly, limited perceptions of relations mean limited consciousness, and greater perceptions of relative conditions bring greater consciousness. Evolution is thus observed to be in the direction of increased perceptions, that is, to be moving toward greater consciousness. Therefore, as evolution continues, consciousness expands; and as evolution advances toward infinity, the perceptions increase, until absolute consciousness is approached.

In the same way, lower forms of life than man have perceptions of the narrower world in which they live, and these constitute the basis of their actions. But man has not only perception of his immediate environment, he can recall in memory many of these external perceptions and combine them in a new order. Such a complex mental grouping is called a concept. Concepts, in turn, combine into the larger group we call knowledge, which is thus seen to rest upon experience-gained perceptions, grouped in memory.

Even though we gain the knowledge from books, it is nevertheless gained by experience; for to read another's writing is an experience as truly as if one were to feel in himself the physical sensations of the writer. Such an experience is, of course, mental rather than physical; but it is still an experience. Reasoning, also, is an experience, arising from the comparison of relations held in memory. In very truth we have no knowledge except that gained through experience, and that experience is a continually increasing consciousness of relations of various perceptions and concepts.

The first form of this consciousness is decidedly limited; for as a new-born babe I possess scarcely more than the instinct inherent in all life to struggle for existence. To what extent these inherited instincts and tendencies depend upon previous experiences of the soul before birth in human form does not concern us now. Enough that I, together with all living beings, have an instinct to sustain existence. This instinct leads to actions that supply nourishment to the body, and these actions register impressions on the consciousness. At this time, I am unaware of more than a few primitive sensations, and my consciousness has a very limited scope. But limited as it is, there soon develops a dim perception of relations. Thus I become aware that the sensation I later call hunger is appeased by taking nourishment, and that certain actions on my part lead to this nourishment being furnished by my mother.

Here I take my first step in positive knowledge; for I have discovered the relation existing between two sets of sensations.

All knowledge possible to me, here and hereafter, must rest upon a similar basis; for there is no knowledge that does not rest upon experience, and no experience apart from a perception of relations.

In this typical case I find that a certain set of sensations is followed by another set of sensations. The same thing happens over and over again, until the connection is established in memory. Because of the repeated association of these two sets of sensations in my experience I conclude that the first set is always followed by the other set. This is KNOWLEDGE.

Growing from infancy to childhood, my perception of relations gains a wider scope. Day by day I add to the store of such experiences, and of others. Some objects have thus attracted my attention through the sense of sight, and I have discovered that things thus seen have come into my possession when reached for. So I reach for the object of my desire. Since my experience so far has been very limited, my knowledge is only partial and I reach for an object across the room with the same assurance as if it were near at hand. But I am unable to procure it, and this adds to my experience.

Later I learn, by repetition of this experience, and comparison of it with similar experiences in which I have successfully gained possession of the coveted object, that some objects are close at hand and others are distant. Thus I correct my first impression that reaching brings an object within range of the sense of touch, and a knowledge of the relation called distance enters my mind. This knowledge is emphasized and made important to me through the sensations of pleasure and pain.

Illustrating the function of pleasure and pain, when learning to walk if I reach for a chair that is too far away, expecting it to support me, I fall and am hurt. But if I am correct in my estimate of distance, I avoid the pain of falling and take pleasure in my achievement. Pleasure and pain, when applied by Nature rather than by man, always are educational; never reward and punishment as society conceives them. (See lesson No. 212.)

Again, a lighted candle looks very pretty and inviting, and I desire to gain impressions of it through other senses than the sense of sight. I expect a pleasurable sensation to follow touching or tasting it, because it is pleasing to the eye. But in this instance my knowledge is imperfect, and the result is pain. Therefore, after touching the lighted candle I revise my opinion of it, and decide that while it is pleasant to sight, it is painful to both touch and taste. And in later years I can form the generalization that acting upon imperfect knowledge often brings some painful result. This is TRUTH.

We now see that Truth is the conformity of cognition to reality. And while at this early age my limited experience causes me to form many erroneous conclusions from the impressions reaching me from the universe, a wider range of experience enables me to revise my early conclusions and approach more nearly the truth. Thus is growth in consciousness the continued approximation of cognition to reality, casting away that which proves erroneous, and confirming that which proves consistent.

In later life there are experiences of a mental nature by which the result of other person's experiences are conveyed to me through speech and writing. Even a thought, however, is a movement in some substance, and implies a perception of relations. The process, therefore, of following the reasoning of another is an experience as truly as is physical action. And I find that through mental effort I can draw conclusions regarding the probable result of a certain course of action. I myself have never had the experience derived from such actions in my own life, but I can compare them with those which I have had which are most like them. If the resultant conclusions are correct, if they parallel reality, I derive benefit from them; but if they are erroneous I suffer. When I have taken this step I rely more upon mental experience to furnish me the necessary knowledge.

But whether the experience be mental or physical, we have but one reason to rely upon it; which is that it furnishes us with more or less accurate data for future action.

It is only because we have found, in a similar way, that we can more or less clearly anticipate conditions and profit by that anticipation that we learn to rely upon the processes of the mind. Sense impressions and reason are thus alike valuable only in so far as they furnish correct knowledge; for upon this depends the ability of the organism continuously to adapt itself to environment, and upon this ability depends its survival. Failure to adapt itself to an environment accurately apprehended and correctly reasoned upon means first pain, and finally death. On the other hand, continuous adaptation means continued life, and the more perfect the adaptation the fuller the life.

Man, then, has found that reason based upon the perceptions of his physical senses is necessary for adaptation and consequent survival; but its value depends upon their accuracy. Therefore, if some other means can be discovered that will give more accurate results, or additional information, progress demands its adoption.

The Proper Test of Either Physical or Psychical Faculties. —That such other faculties exist in nature —faculties which, relied upon bring satisfactory results—needs but a glance about us to demonstrate. For example, the homing pigeon needs neither reason nor any past experience of the region over which it flies to find its way unerringly to its roost, hundreds of strange miles away. And a honey-bee needs neither reason nor compass to take a straight course to its hive through forests and over mountains. The oriole also needs no previous experience to enable it to build its cleverly-woven hanging nest. These and many other instincts of wild creatures are reliable within their boundaries, just as man's reason is reliable within certain limits. Experience alone determines in any case how much reliance can be placed on either; and this conformity of later experience to expected results alone is the test of the value of any faculty.

To learn thus to check the reports of the senses by experience—to test in the laboratory of life the accuracy of observation and the conclusions based thereon; especially to be able to do this mentally, without going through the slow and usually painful process of physical testing—is the greater part of wisdom.

Early in his life the great sage, Giordano Bruno, found out this truth. Looking across the undulating foothills to Mt. Vesuvius,[1] apparently scarred and bare of all vegetation, he desired greatly to visit the volcano and observe its barren stretches at close range. Finally the opportunity came for him to take the journey and he set forth from his native fields and vineyards. What was his surprise on reaching the distant mountain to find its sides covered with vegetation, while, looking back on the lands of his fathers from that distance, they seemed as barren and destitute of life as the mountain had seemed. This lesson was never forgotten.

From it he learned to distrust the reports of his senses, and thereafter carefully devised means of checking and testing the accuracy of all sense impressions. As a result he became the greatest scientist of his time and assisted in the overthrow of the Aristotelian system of philosophy and the establishment of the Heliocentric system of Astronomy, by his achievements proving that he had found the true method of Wisdom.

His greatness was directly connected with the fact that he early discovered what we must all discover before we can correct and improve our knowledge—

namely, that we constantly misinterpret our sense impressions, and despite repeated efforts to check them one against another and to subject them to reason we almost daily draw from their reports wrong conclusions.

Thus we see a familiar face across the street and go to offer greetings only to find ourselves confronted by an utter stranger. We have made a mistake. Or we hear a sound, and conclude it comes from a great distance; but investigation proves it to be a faint sound close at hand that, because of lack of volume, we mistook for a greater sound, more remote.

But in addition to the reports received by these physical senses, we have to consider the claims of the super-physical senses; for some people declare they are able to check the impressions of the physical senses by impressions received through other avenues. They also assert that they are able to draw correct conclusions without the ordinary process of reasoning. Both the truth and the reliability of such impressions and conclusions must be subjected to the same tests. Their value—like the value of more usual conclusions—can be determined only by experience.

We have just found that our only excuse for accepting the reports of the physical senses and ordinary reason as a basis for action is that conclusions based upon them have coincided with later experience. The reliability and truth of other methods of interpreting phenomena must be determined by the same standard.

Thus if by some other faculty than physical sight I see a friend approaching, and later this friend actually pays me a visit, and I ascertain he was on the way at the time I had the vision, I tentatively conclude there is an inner sense of sight. If I have frequent experiences of this kind, as some persons certainly do, and if on each occasion when I see the event by clairvoyant vision, the external event actually transpires, though I had no means of knowing, through any physical avenue, that it would so transpire, I am gradually justified in placing confidence in such visions as a basis of future action.

If, again, some business proposition is presented to me and even before I have reasoned about the matter I feel that it will prove a failure, and events later prove this Intuition correct; and such occurrences frequently take place, I am justified in concluding that there is a possibility of arriving at a correct judgment apart from reasoning. And if on many occasions I find the experience with reality coincides with the impressions received through intuition, I am justified in basing future actions upon intuition.

If in such a case the report of physical sight or ordinary reason conflicts with the inner sense of sight, and with Intuition, I must then reflect which has more generally proved correct in the past, and incline toward that one.

The Dogmatism of Material Scientists. —It should be unnecessary to call attention to the foregoing obvious truths. But there is a tendency among material scientists to overlook the fact that the physical senses are but instruments by which reality may be determined, and that their value lies wholly in their ability correctly to report the universe and to direct man's actions in conformity therewith.

To assert, as many of them do, that the physical senses and reason are the only means by which the universe may be apprehended and knowledge gained, is thoroughly unscientific; for any such assertion is an assumption not verified by experience.

When it takes this attitude, material science is as dogmatic as the religions it ridicules; for it assumes a superiority and infallibilty that its own history refutes. It boasts of its experimental methods, but fails to apply those methods except to a very limited section of the universe—a limited section which it dogmatically assumes to be the only legitimate field of investigation. When scientists take such an unwarranted stand, sincere men, seeking the truth in all regions; seeking, that is, to conform cognition to the infinite and inexhaustible Reality, must protest.

Attempts like this to narrow the field of inquiry arise from a very natural effort to bring the subject of study—this vast universe—within reach of the circumscribed intelligence of the investigator.

It is not a new attempt. The Inquisition rose to a similar attempt, and haled before it, a few hundred years ago, the famous scientist, Galileo, who had dared to investigate beyond the ecclesiastical limits and to inquire into the solar system. Such breadth of inquiry was then held sacrilegious, just as the breadth of inquiry of Psychical Research and still more of Occultism is subject to the reproach of orthodox physical scientists. For while today the legitimate field of experimental investigation has expanded to include the entire realm of physical phenomena, it is still restricted to that comparatively limited field, and those who declare that there are vaster realms to be explored, interior to the physical, are considered to be as foolish as were the first astronomers who declared the earth to be, not the center of the universe, but merely one planet among many, moving around a sun a million times larger.

Yet since we agree that all knowledge must be based upon experience, and since repeated experiences, as we have just seen, tend to correct false impressions derived from a too-limited experience, it is clear that any avenue by which man can arrive at that wider and more accurate cognition is legitimate, and that the only test of its usefulness lies in the verity.

Thus if I have a dream, and this dream is followed in a few days by a certain event, and I have the same dream again and again, and on each occasion it is followed by the same event, the dream is just as useful a source of information regarding the approach of this particular event as if the information had come through some recognized physical channel.

If such dreaming is cultivated and the images thus presented to the mind are found by experience invariably to signify approaching events, and by this means situations are foretold accurately and repeatedly that could not have been known by any merely physical means, these dreams become a legitimate source of valuable knowledge, whose reliability has been determined by repeated experiment.

As a matter of fact, many people receive information through such dreams, and there are indisputable records of lives having been saved by them.

True, I am not justified in coming to the conclusion that dreams, clairvoyance, telepathy, and other psychic activities now called occult, are to be relied upon without full proof; and I am not justified in accepting loose explanations of them; or any explanations that have not been tested thoroughly by experiments.

Thus if I hear a voice clairaudiently, purporting to come from someone long since dead, I may accept the fact that I hear the voice and wait for further confirmation of its supposed source. Devices have been arranged to check physical experiments against false conclusions; and tests may be contrived in these cases also to preclude the possibility of deception in determining the identity of a discarnate entity. Nor am I justified in following the advice received through this clairaudient faculty unless I have found through repeated observation of information so gained that it is reliable. Even then, on some particular occasions the information gained might lead astray, just as I might find the advice of a friend unusually good, but on some special occasion it would prove faulty. The accuracy and value of information received through any channel, physical or psychical, equally requires experimental determination.

The literature covering the field of psychical research, here just touched upon, will prove amply to any unprejudicated mind that there are senses and faculties other than the five physical senses.

Physical science, as yet unable to account for these powers, conveniently ignores them, and, assuming an air of enlightened superiority, puts the entire matter aside by simply saying "Bosh!" This is bad enough, as an exhibition of the limitations of our advanced men of science, but it is worse because to the lay mind the utterances of these savants are considered final.

The general impression is that material science is infallible, when the truth is that it is undergoing a constant process of revision, each decade trying to correct the mistakes of the previous decade. Thus what is accepted as scientific today was unknown a few years ago, and may in its turn be refuted in years to come. Indeed, many of the very things science proclaimed to be impossible thirty years ago are now accomplished facts. Current scientific opinion is thus continually overthrown by new discoveries, and the whole structure must be rebuilt to conform to the altered conceptions.

This is not at all to the discredit of material science, and occult science should follow the same procedure; for, as we have been seeing, it conforms to the method by which knowledge grows; but nevertheless to build upon the conclusions of material science alone is to build upon the ever-shifting sands. Its conclusions should be steadied and bettered by the binding cement brought from other and wider regions.

Super-physical Faculties.—But whatever the value of the conclusions of others, every true scien-

tist after assimilating them, desires to read the Book
of Nature for himself. Sooner or later he examines
the ground of his own first-hand knowledge, and
here he well may start with the positive knowledge
"I AM." This, certainly, he knows of himself.

Next, he discovers there is something else than
I AM: The Universe Exists. This he Feels.

It is from these feelings that he endeavors to
determine the nature of that universe in relation to
himself; to the one who feels and knows. And here
he discovers the dimly-felt presence of the super-
physical senses and is almost sure to learn that in
his community is someone claiming to possess these
senses in a more marked form.

Through this person, or others of the same sort,
the earnest scientist supplements the knowledge
gained from physical research with the further
knowledge to be gained from psychical research. It
is probable that his first experiments will be incon-
clusive; but if he persists over a sufficiently extensive
area, he will discover beyond the shadow of a doubt
—as has every scientist who has done thorough
work in this field—that there assuredly are faculties,
principles, and forces as yet undreamed of by ma-
terialistic philosophers. With this conviction he becomes an occult scientist.

The Inadequacies of Physical Science. — Already
in the realm of physical science he has found its
advocates making claim to knowledge they can in no
way substantiate. He knows that the things con-
ceded to be the very bulwarks of scientific accuracy

and precision are very far from it when put to the test.

Such discrepancies between theory and practice are not loudly announced to the general public, because the bread and butter of scientific men depend upon their reputation for knowledge and accuracy. For example, the Law of Gravitation, which is the basis of all astronomical and mechanical reckoning, and is stated thus—The attraction of Gravity between two bodies is directly in proportion to the product of their masses and inversely as the square of their distance—does not give precision in celestial calculations. By all the teachings of physical science the planets should exert an influence upon each other which could be exactly measured according to this law. But as a matter of experience it is found that a decimal must be added to the squares of their disstances, and even with this tampering with figures to make the answer coincide with observed results the actual positions of the planets continue to vary from their calculated places, and there is a continual alteration of the mathematical formulas in an attempt to get the correct answer.

Again, take the theory of the tides as accepted and taught in the schools of the land. One might suppose, from the definite way it is set forth, that this theory is the essence of scientific accuracy. But in actual practice the tides do not at all coincide with their theoretical rise and fall;[2] indeed, the divergence is sometimes so wide that the Moon apparently repels the tides instead of attracting them,[3] and they occur at points almost opposite those at which they would theoretically be calculated. Therefore in actually predetermining the tides for practical purposes their fluctuations are frankly calculated from past observations. It is the case of getting the right answer without knowing why, like a schoolboy working a problem whose answer is given in the back of the book.

Noting this familiar performance on the part of men of standing in the scientific world, our occult investigator is not surprised to find that there are many claims advanced by enthusiastic students of occultism also that can not be verified. But he no more throws over all of occultism when he makes this disconcerting discovery, than, under similar circumstances, he casts aside all the findings of physical science.

The Proof of the Pudding Is in the Eating.— At this stage, his attention may be called to Astrology. No one can seriously and thoroughly investigate this occult science without becoming convinced that certain positions of the planets coincide with certain characteristics and events in the life of men.

No psychic sense is needed for such a demonstration. It is purely a matter of experiment. For if a certain angular relation of two planets coincides always with events of a certain nature, and enough birth-charts of persons having this position can be secured to prove it to be much more than a coincidence, no amount of theoretical argument can refute the facts.

Physical science is reluctant to accept such conclusions, or even to make the necessary experiments to verify them, because it has so far found no adequate theory to account for them. Isabel M. Lewis, of the U. S. Naval Observatory, writing in *Nature Magazine* for April, 1931, says: "It is doubtful, indeed, if any astronomer would know how to cast a horoscope or make astrological predictions of any kind." (See lesson No. 169.) Yet these same astronomers, ignorant even of how to set up a birthchart, freely pass judgment that astrology must be false because they have no theoretical grounds by which to explain it.

Alchemy may next claim the attention of our investigator. Although he knows it is stigmatized as an exploded science, he no longer accepts as final the dictum of a school he has found to be often prejudiced, a dictum, moreover, pronounced by men without knowledge of the subject they condemn. He finds that the two chief tenets of Alchemy, as laid down by the ancients, are that there is a Primitive First Substance of which all physical matter is composed, and that it is possible to transmute one or more metals into another totally distinct metal.

Such ideas have been ridiculed by chemists until within the last few years. Now, however, it has been proved that all atoms are built up in a special way of particles of electricity, some negatively charged, others equally positively charged, all held within a certain volume by the interaction of the attraction between the negative electrons and the positive positrons. Thus has electricity been demonstrated as the Primitive First Substance.

Furthermore, radium decays into helium and lead. Professor Ramsey has transmuted copper into lithium; and other scientists, through bombarding the atoms of one or two elements, much as radium bombards on its own, occasionally score a direct hit and smash out a piece of the nucleus of the element and thereby transmute each part into an atom of some other element. Thus the very theory and processes of Alchemy, so long scoffed at by material scientists, have now been demonstrated in their own laboratories.

By methods as experimental as theirs, under conditions as strictly scientific, the Occult Scientist has demonstrated Magic, Astrology, and Alchemy. This makes him reluctant to discard any branch of occultism without first giving it a thorough investigation.

He approaches different methods of Divination with, perhaps, a good deal of skepticism; but even in this he is surprised to find results that can not be attributed to coincidence, and he is forced to conclude that there are laws underlying such matters totally ignored by physical science. But then, he reflects, physical science has never determined the laws governing the source of the sun's heat. Every theory it has formulated to account for this phenomenon— and, for that matter, for numerous others—has been torn to shreds by later investigation. It is not astonishing, then, that it has failed to discover the mental laws governing Divination.

But just as the true scientist finds the material sciences oppressed by many erroneous ideas and theories, so also he finds speculation and supposition so largely covering the facts of occult science that he can gain very little through reading the current works upon such subjects.

Mystical folly and absurd and conflicting doctrines meet him on every hand. Everyone whom he consults has an opinion, but usually quite unsupported by experimental facts. His only recourse seems to be to advance, step by step, applying the methods of experimental science to psychical and spiritual things, and so gain knowledge at first hand. He knows that to do this requires application, effort, keen discrimination and, finally, the development of the senses of the unconscious mind.

Although intuition and thought transference undoubtedly are activities or perceptions of the unconscious mind, because they so commonly reported the phenomena of the physical plane the ancients classified them as physical senses, along with the other five. But whether five or seven, the experience gained through these physical senses is the foundation of all knowledge of physical life.

The Seven Psychic Senses.—There are also seven psychic senses by which the phenomena of the world interior to the physical are reported to the unconscious mind, and from thence may be raised into the region of physical consciousness. The experience gained through the use of these psychic senses is the foundation of knowledge of life on the inner planes. Nor are they so rare as to make this manner of investigation a practical impossibility; for more people than is generally supposed possess at least one of them in a more or less advanced stage of development.

The number is unknown because the ridicule that follows the announcement that one possesses such a faculty frequently deters people from making their psychic ability known. Nevertheless, even a little candid investigation will reveal the fact that such senses exist, and that by their use worlds other than the physical may be explored and understood, even as the physical world is explored and understood through the reports of the physical senses.

Moreover, even as the physical senses may be developed to a state of keenness and accuracy, so may the psychic senses be roused from their dormant condition and be educated to a state of efficiency.

In this education, either one of two methods may be followed. One is negative, mediumistic, passive and destructive to the individuality. It brings a train of evil results and should never be allowed. The other method is positive, controlling, active, and tends to build up the Will and Individuality, increasing the power of the mentality and bringing greater vigor to the body.

Psychic Senses Are Not Infallible. —This constructive method of training brings highly satisfactory results, and may be followed without danger. Moreover, as the psychic senses develop, their reports should be carefully analyzed and verified. They are yet immature, and as it took years after birth to educate the sense of sight so that it became a reliable guide to effort, it may take that long to develop psychic-sight, or any psychic sense, to a comparative degree of accuracy.

Most persons' psychic senses when first awakened are just about as accurate as were their physical senses immediately after birth. Consequently it is absurd to take the reports of these rudimentary faculties as indisputable. Yet they can be developed through exercise; and experience will indicate just how much reliability can be placed upon their reports.

It will be found that they often give information that later can be verified — such information as could not possibly be gained at the time through the physical senses. And as the reliability of the psychic senses increases they may safely be used to report the phenomena of the inner worlds. These reports may be checked, one against another, and compared with later experiences of those realms in such a way as to give the same certainty about the things of the inner worlds as may be had through the physical senses about the things of the outer world.

At a still later period of occult development, if the student has had the patience and ability to follow so far the royal road leading to initiation, it becomes possible to leave the physical body consciously and travel on a plane interior to the physical.

Means may be devised by which it is possible to prove with scientific certainty that this journey was an actual fact, and that the places thus visited were actually entered. When he makes such a journey, the student is able to say with certainty that there are inner regions, just as when he visits a city on the physical plane he is certain that such a city exists, and can describe it.

Immortality is more difficult of proof. Still, one who visits the homes of the dead and converses with them has ample assurance of life after death.

In our experience with the material world we have often found the instincts implanted by Nature a better index to reality than reasoning from limited premises; so in this matter also we find our instincts a better guide than prejudice. Thus, instinct teaches animals to prepare warm dens for winter and stock them with food. They do not know of winter by individual experience, for they make this preparation for the first winter of life. Similarly, man instinctively looks for a future life and strives to prepare for it. The occultist, urged on by instinct, prepares for a life immortal, a life of never-ending progression; and by the development of his individual faculties explores its realms, and while yet on earth gains knowledge of its laws.

We repeat that the data upon which occult science rests is purely experimental, and even as in physical science it is necessary to form a hypothesis as a working basis, so also in occult science certain working hypotheses are essential. But occult science does not stand or fall by the correctness of theories any more than does physical science.

For example, the science of chemistry was founded upon Dalton's Atomic Theory, until recently universally accepted. But with the explosion of that theory which so long served as a working hypothesis for all chemists, and the adoption of the Electronic Theory in its stead, chemistry does not fall.

Neither does the disproof of any prevalent occult theory seriously affect occultism. Its truths are based upon observed phenomena carefully checked and compared. Yet when some ideas not sufficiently checked and confirmed are admitted to the edifice, they can be removed or improved without destroying the whole structure.

We Make No Claim to Infallibility. — Every science and every religion of the past which has claimed infallibility has lived to see such claim disproved. In the very nature of things, as I trust I have clearly shown, any claim to infallibility is absurd; because knowledge of the universe is endless and the evolution of intelligence is toward the acquisition of more and more knowledge.

Nor are we attempting to get our ideas accepted on faith. On the contrary, we indicate to the student just how to go about it to develop his own intelligence and his own psychic faculties, and earnestly advise him to disprove or verify every statement we make by experiments of his own.

Most religions teach that there is a life after death. But they discourage any attempt to prove such an existence. We, THE CHURCH OF LIGHT, however, believe that painstaking research should be carried out on every possible plane, and in all departments of nature, including those physical and those spiritual, to the end that man may not merely believe, but may know, the conditions under which he is required to live in each distinct realm, that he may utilize the laws and principles so discovered to be successful, in the larger sense, wherever he may function.

Physical life is but a fragment of that total life which is man's inheritance. The more knowledge we have of the laws of the physical plane, including occult laws, the surer our chances of physical success. Physical success is not to be ignored.

But we must also, if we are to have a basis for success in our life in its vaster scope, acquire a knowledge of the laws governing other planes. The more comprehensive our knowledge, the better we are fitted to adjust ourselves to the demands of this wider life. It is this knowledge that THE RELIGION OF THE STARS attempts to furnish.

These lessons make no claim to infallibility. They do, however, present the present views of those on various planes, including the physical, who anciently or in modern times, have been specially qualified for, and have carried out, research on every available plane. They are offered to students, therefore, not as the final word after which nothing more can be said; but drawing from high intelligences on various planes, as the best information available at the present moment of evolution.

---

[1]Giordano Bruno, His Life, Thought, and Martyrdom, by William Boulting.

[2]Young's General Astronomy, 307.

[3]The Tides, by George Darwin, 161, 188.

ASTRAL SUBSTANCE

Serial No. 40

THE CHURCH OF LIGHT
Box 1525, Los Angeles 53, California

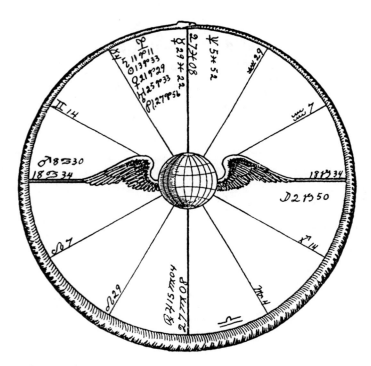

SARAH STANLEY GRIMKE, April 3, 1850, 11:03 a.m. 76:30W.
43:30N.

Writer (Mercury in 10th), astrologer (Uranus in 10th) and daring pioneer (5 planets in Aries) in placing The Brotherhood of
Light teachings before the world. Assisted T. H. Burgoyne in writing that part of Light of Egypt, Vol. I, which deals with The
Science of the Stars, and in many other ways gave valuable co-
operation (Pluto in 10th trine Moon, ruler of 1st) in spreading The
Brotherhood of Light teachings.

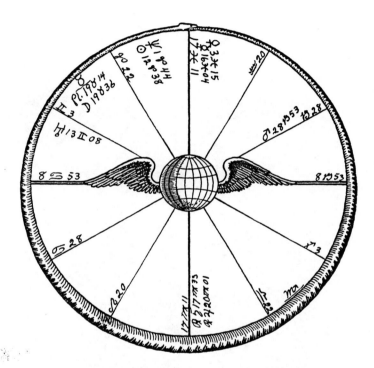

PROFESSOR NICHOLAS MURRAY BUTLER, April 2, 1862, 10:30 a.m. 74:15W. 40:35N.

Attended universities both in America and abroad (Mercury and Venus in 9th, ruling long journeys and teaching). Has been president (Sun in 10th) of Columbia University (Mercury conjunction M.C.) since 1902. Has held prominent offices in industrial companies (Sun conjunction Neptune in 10th, sextile Uranus). Chairman of Republican National Convention at various times (Sun in 10th in Aries tends to politics, Moon in house of friends trine Jupiter gives popularity).

ASTRAL SUBSTANCE

PHYSICAL science has now moved to a position where it fully endorses the dictum of the old alchemists that all existence is composed of the "first matter." Mass and energy are convertible, each into the other. To quote from The Evolution of Physics (1938), by Albert Einstein and Leopold Infeld: "Mass is energy and energy has mass. The two conservation laws of mass and energy are combined by the relativity theory into one, the conservation law of mass-energy." The conversion of matter into energy provides a tremendous force which, as so-called atomic energy, may in the future be used to destroy much of mankind, or harnessed by industry may provide many necessities and luxuries of a new and higher civilization.

In addition to matter, which is one aspect of energy, physics also must deal with field. There are, for instance, the gravitational field between material particles, and electric fields and magnetic fields. To quote further from The Evolution of Physics, "Field represents energy, matter represents mass. . . . We could therefore say: Matter is where the concentration of energy is great, field where the concentration of energy is small. But if this is the case, then the difference between matter and field is a quantitative rather than a qualitative one. There is no sense in regarding matter and field as two qualities quite different from each other. We cannot imagine a definite surface separating distinctly field and matter."

"What impresses our senses as matter is really a great concentration of energy into comparatively small space." The energy thus concentrated has the properties of positive and negative charges of electricity. The positive electric charge, or particle, having a mass equal to that of the electron, and a charge of the same magnitude but differing in sign, is called a positron. The negative electric charge, or particle, having a mass equal to that of the positron, and a charge of the same magnitude but differing in sign, is called an electron. These two electrical particles are the bricks from which all matter is built.

A positron and an electron when united have weight, but are electrically neutral. The prevalent theory at the present time is that the nucleus of an atom contains heavy neutral pieces of matter, formed by the union of positrons and electrons held together by the interaction of the attraction between the negative electrons and the positive positrons — about 1848 units of weight—tied up closely with a positron whose weight is one unit and whose electrical charge is plus one. Such a combination of positive and negative charges constitute a proton. All atoms of matter have at their core one or more proton.

In 1932, Chadwick discovered that in addition to protons at the nucleus of an atom, there may be other particles built up of positrons and electrons much as are the protons, but containing an additional electron, so that they are electrically neutral and weigh

1849 units. These are neutrons, which because they bear no electrical charge, when they are used to bombard other atoms easily penetrate to their nuclei. Atoms having the same number of free electrons, and thus the same chemical properties, may have in their nuclei a different number of neutrons, and thus a different atomic mass. Such atomic twins are called isotopes.

The positive charge on the proton of an atom is balanced by the negative charge on an electron which revolves in an elliptical orbit around the nucleus of which the proton forms a part. Each atom has an equal number of protons and free revolving electrons, and thus is electrically neutral.

The electrons that revolve around the nucleus of an atom—which contains protons and may contain neutrons—much as the planets revolve around the sun, are arranged in zones. There are not more than two electrons revolving in the zone next to the nucleus, not more than eight in the second zone, and not more than eight in the third zone. Zones farther out may have more than eight electrons. It is the arrangement of these revolving electrons which determines the chemical properties of an atom.

Although two of the chemical elements had not been isolated until 1947, the atomic table listed 92 different elements. Hydrogen, the lightest element, and number 1 in the table, has 1 free electron revolving in an orbit about its nucleus. The next heaviest element, helium, has 2 free electrons revolving around its nucleus; lithium, the third heaviest has 3;

beryllium, the fourth heaviest element has 4, and uranium, the heaviest element found in a natural state, with an atomic weight of 238.5, has 92 electrons revolving in its outer region. The synthetically produced neptunium has 93, the synthetically produced plutonium has 94, the synthetically produced americuim has 95, and the synthetically produced curium has 96.

By bombarding ordinary uranium with neutrons it is possible to produce neptunium and plutonium. Plutonium and the uranium isotope U235 have a tendency to fission. Bombarding ordinary uranium (U238) gives the uranium isotope U239 plus energy. This isotope is radioactive, and one-half the quantity thus obtained will change into neptunium in 23 minutes. Neptunium is also radioactive, and one-half of it will then change into plutonium in 2.3 days. In the fission of either unanium 235 or plutonium, a chain reaction results through the release of other neutrons which bombard other nuclei. Once the process is started it continues until the whole mass is broken down into other elements. The sum of the separate weights of the resulting particles is different than the weight of the parent particle. This means that matter is converted into energy. In the explosion of U235 or plutonium, only one-tenth of one per cent of matter is thus converted into what is commonly called atomic energy. The problem at this writing is to find a method of controlling the fission of plutonium, so its energy may be released slowly and provide power for the wheels of industry.

In addition to field, where energy concentration is so great that it is commonly called matter, science has observed that energy moves across vast regions of space and exerts an influence. Just how the sun holds the earth in its orbit, and with the moon influences the tides, has so far not been explained. The law of gravitation discovered by Newton states that any particle of matter attracts any other particle with a force proportional inversely to the square of the distance between them, and directly to the product of their masses. But the process by which one particle thus reaches out across space, or through some material obstacle, to attract the other particle is as yet unknown.

Not only do the sun, planets and stars reach across empty space to influence the earth and other orbs through gravitational pull, but they radiate light and radiant heat and other forms of electromagnetism which in some manner traverse vast space. How does the sun reach across 93 million empty miles to light our days? How does its warmth traverse 93 million miles to keep earth's temperature genial enough to encourage vegetable and animal growth?

To account for these and other electromagnetic phenomena science invented the ether. The ether was frictionless, it penetrated everything. It sheared into positive and negative electrical particles. It carried, by means of its waves, radiant heat, light, radio waves, and other electromagnetic energy across space, and in the case of radio waves through the walls of your home where they are picked up and the modulations they carry are amplified by your radio set to give you information and enjoyment.

The tendency of advanced physics now is to forget the ether and try to explain all phenomena, including matter, gravitation and electromagnetic waves in terms of field. All are supposed to be characteristic distortions of space. Space takes the place of the ether. However, this new conception still holds un-solved problems. To quote once more from The Evolution of Physics:

"The theory of relativity stresses the importance of the field concept in physics. But we have not yet succeeded in formulating a pure field physics. For the present we must still assume the existence of both: field and matter."

It is not unlikely that in due course of time radio waves will be commonly mentioned as distortions of space. But in common parlance radio programs come over the ether.

Not only so, but recent text books on physics still refer to the ether. The most recent such text book to which I have access is Simplified Physics, by Sidney Aylmer Small and Charles Ramsey Clark, published in 1943. It gives the prevailing present view:

"When things take place in presumably empty space we must assume that empty space is not empty, that a vacuum has something in it. To this material that our senses cannot detect but that our intellects demand in order that we may think about light and wireless we give the name of the ether or simply ether.

"The ether, then, is something pervading all materials and space, even that space which to our senses seems empty. It transmits heat, light, chemical energy and wireless waves. It when stressed or strained produces magnetism and when sheared (sliced) forms positive and negative charges of electricity."

Because electromagnetism transmits energy from the outer plane to the inner plane, and from the inner plane to the outer plane, the ether will repeatedly be referred to throughout Brotherhood of Light lessons. It would be awkward each time to speak instead of distortions of space, and confusing to most readers who are unfamiliar with relativity and the field theory. But the reader who is familiar with relativity and the field theory can substitute certain warpings of space when etheric energy is mentioned, and different warpings of space when astral substance is mentioned. And his conceptions will probably be more precise. But for most it is easier to think of matter, not as space distorted in one way, radio waves as space distorted in another way, and the mental image of a cow as space distorted in still another manner. It is much easier for the ordinary individual to think of any existence in terms of substance.

Even the relativists and those most enthusiastic about the field theory of existence still sanction the use of the word ether as it will be employed in Brotherhood of Light lessons. To quote once again from The Evolution of Physics:

"Our only way out seems to be to take for granted the fact that space has the physical property of transmitting electromagnetic waves, and not to bother too much about the meaning of this statement. We may still use the word ether, but only to express some physical property of space. The word ether has changed its meanings many times in the development of science. At the moment it no longer stands for a medium built up of particles. Its story, by no means finished, is continued by the relativity theory."

The most essential difference between that which is commonly referred to as etheric energy and physical energy is its velocity. Things having low velocities have the properties of physical things. But as velocities increase these properties undergo marked change. As velocities increase time slows down, the length of an object decreases in the direction of its movement, and its mass increases. These results postulated by the Special Theory of Relativity have been tested experimentally and are now universally accepted by those highest in the ranks of physical science.

At the velocity of light an object or an energy acquires some remarkable properties. Commonly, for instance, the walls of our homes keep objects out; but radio waves having their origin a thousand miles away have no difficulty in coming into the room in which we sit. In empty space they have the velocity of light, 186,284 miles per second (1942).

But there is another group of commonly observed phenomena which cannot be explained either by the properties of physical substance or by the properties of electromagnetic energies. Scientists term these the psi phenomena. Psi phenomena embrace all the phenomena covered by the terms extra-sensory perception and all the phenomena covered by the term psychokinetic effect.

Extra-sensory perception embraces all means of acquiring information in which the physical senses or reason are not involved, such as clairvoyance, clairaudience, telepathy, precognition and postcognition. The psychokinetic effect, or psychokinesis, embraces those phenomena in which physical things are moved or influenced without any physical or electromagnetic contact with them. The influencing of mechanically released dice to come to rest with the faces up which had been decided upon, which is the test commonly used in university experiments to prove the existence of this phenomenon, and the influence of planetary energies over human life and other life are examples of psychokinesis. All psi phenomena are due to inner-plane energies.

It was the Special Theory of Relativity, followed to its practical and logical conclusions which led to the discovery of releasing and utilizing atomic energy. And it is this same Special Theory of Relativity followed to its practical and logical conclusions which indicates both how inner-plane energies operate and what can be done to cause them to work more to the individual's advantage.

This theory postulates that at the velocity of light an object loses all its length, time stands still, and gravitation loses its power. Therefore, on the inner plane where velocity is greater than light, time, distance and gravitation are of a quite different order than they are on the physical plane. And innumerable experiments carried out in various universities prove that this is actually the case.

By 1947, Duke University Laboratory alone had conducted over one-million trials of extra-sensory perception; other university laboratories, following similar methods had reported over two-million trials, and there were something over a million trials, with responses from over 46,000 subjects made by the Zenith radio program in the winter of 1937-38.

These experiments indicate that, as the Special Theory of Relativity carried to its logical conclusion indicates, on the inner plane where velocities are greater than that of light, not only the Now can be perceived, but consciousness can move either forward or backward along world-lines. Moving backward, it can perceive happenings of the past. Moving forward it can perceive happenings of the future.

One of the serious difficulties now confronting university experimenters is to devise methods by which precognitive clairvoyance can be separated from pure telepathy. It is recognized that perceiving things as they will exist in the future is relatively common. Therefore, if a record is made of the sender's thought at the time the subject makes his call, there is no proof that the information was not obtained through clairvoyantly seeing this record, rather than through telepathy. And if any objective record is ever made of the sender's thought after it is sent, there is no proof that the information was not obtained through perceiving this record as it will exist in the future.

The university experiments indicate also, as the Special Theory of Relativity carried to its logical conclusion indicates, that distance has no effect upon inner-plane perception. Both clairvoyance and telepathy experiments indicate that, other things being equal, it is as easy to get a telepathic message, or to witness an event clairvoyantly, when the distance is a hundred miles or a thousand miles, as when the distance is only that separating two rooms in the same building.

Furthermore, as the Special Theory of Relativity carried to its logical conclusion indicates, on the inner plane where velocities are greater than that of light, gravitation loses its influence on things. Along with the experiments on extra-sensory perception, various universities have been conducting experiments also with the psychokinetic effect. And they have proved by exhaustive experiments that the mind, operating through space, can influence physical objects, such as the fall of mechanically released dice, in a predetermined way.

The mind and thoughts of the individual exerting this influence are not physical. They belong to the inner, or astral, plane. If one thinks of a cloud or of a star, no effort need be made to overcome the influence of gravitation on the thoughts. Nor does it take longer to think of a star which is light-years away than to think of a cloud a few hundred feet above the earth. Yet mind and thought have an existence, and possess energy, or they could not influence physical objects, such as the fall of dice in the psychokinetic tests.

Although the field conception of electromagnetic energies is making the old conceptions of the ether obsolete, it is convenient to refer to ether waves in connection with both light and radio. And if the field conception could be carried far enough, it would probably reveal that mental images, astrological energies, disembodied human beings, and the high-velocity counterparts of all physical things, are other elastic distortions of space. But because people are familiar with substance, and are not familiar with elastic distortions of space, they will be able to grasp the function of electromagnetism better if they think of it as lines of force or waves in etheric substance. And they will be better able to grasp the functions and the properties of the inner plane, where velocities are greater than light, if they think of that region as being composed of astral substance, which is frictionless and which penetrates and moves freely through physical and etheric substances.

This brings us to an extremely important fact confirmed by ample observation. For an inner-plane energy to influence a physical object, or for a physical energy to influence inner-plane conditions, electromagnetic energies—which have approximately the velocity of light—must be present to transmit the energies of one plane to the other. Such electromagnetic energies are generated by every cell of the body,

especially by the nerve and brain cells, and constitute both the nerve currents and the life of the human
form. All psychic phenomena in which there are
physical manifestations are produced through the
utilization of electromagnetic energies by an intelligence operating from the inner plane.

Even the most orthodox psychology now embraces
the idea that man has a subconscious, or unconscious
mind. This unconscious mind, which exists and functions on the inner plane, is composed of the thoughts,
emotions and other states of consciousness which the
individual has experienced in his past. These
thoughts, energized by emotion, have been organized in the unconscious mind according to the Law
of Association. And, as modern psychiatry and
psychoanalysis demonstrate, at all times they exercise a powerful influence over the conscious thoughts,
emotions and behavior.

Not only do the desires of the thought-cells and
thought-cell groups of the unconscious mind largely
determine the individual's thoughts, emotions and
actions, but they also exert psychokinetic power to
mold his physical environment to bring into his life
the conditions and events they desire. The events and
conditions some of these thought-cell groups desire
are beneficial to the individual, but unfortunately the
desires of other thought-cell groups are for conditions and events which are detrimental to the individual.

So long as the individual is unaware of the desires
of the various thought-cell groups within his uncon-

scious mind his power to direct his own destiny is sadly limited. Even though he has a brilliant intellect and exercises excellent reasoning power, the desires of certain groups of thought-cells within his unconscious mind, exercising psychokinetic power may, and often do, attract into his life misfortune. Some of the thought-cell groups may have been so organized in his unconscious mind that they work for, and bring him unusual good fortune where business, or honor or speculation is concerned, and other thought-cell groups may have been so organized that they work for, and bring him miserable health, unhappiness in marriage, and repeated difficulty with his friends.

All Physical Things Have an Astral Counterpart. —Even as all physical objects possess mass, so also do they have an astral, or inner-plane, counterpart. As material scientists are not agreed on the structure of matter, it would be presumptious to go further and describe in detail that of which things on the inner, or astral, plane are composed. It is simpler merely to state they are composed of astral substance, and to state the observed properties of this substance.

While all physical things have an astral counterpart, there are innumerable objects, energies and intelligences on the astral plane which have no physical counterpart. So long as the astral counterpart of any object is bound to it by etheric, or electromagnetic, energies there is an exchange of energies between the physical counterpart and the astral counterpart. The energies having approximately the velocity of light make contact with the low velocities of physical substance and also make contact with the high velocities of astral substance. Through them the physical object transmits energy to, and influences, its astral counterpart, and the astral object transmits energy to, and influences, its physical counterpart.

While the physical also tends to shape the astral counterpart, the most significant relation which commonly exists between physical substance and its astral counterpart is that the astral interpenetrates and has a molding power over the physical.

This astral counterpart also records and retains in its frictionless substance every experience of a life-form. The most outstanding characteristic of astral substance is its responsiveness to the molding power of thought. All life-forms react to environment through an awareness which is recorded in their astral forms. And this record of experiences not only persists and continues to influence the destiny of the life-form, but the strongest such recorded energies impress the astral counterpart of the germ cells, and through this association hand down to subsequent generations racial memories which express as instinct and racial habits and racial physical characteristics.

The astral counterpart exerts a formative influence over all life. It seems quite certain, for instance, that the force which causes a seed to grow into an organism of a certain form and with certain functions does not lie merely in its chemical properties. Nor does it appear to lie in any particular arrangement of its cells; for two vegetable seeds of the same size and apparently of the same chemical and molecular composition, when planted in the same soil may produce plants whose forms and properties are totally dissimilar. Likewise there is very little observable difference in the chemical composition and molecular structure of sperms and germs that generate animals of entirely different species. Though as yet beyond the view of physical science, this formative power that molds every living thing to its proper shape and structure must lie somewhere.

It is now commonly recognized by psychologists that all memory resides in the subconscious, or unconscious mind. This means that memory is recorded in astral substance, and to be recalled by physical consciousness it must utilize electromagnetic energies to impress the physical cells of the brain.

Every theory based upon a material foundation that has so far been advanced to account for memory has been found inadequate. But if we consider that accompanying and interpenetrating the physical brain is another brain of finer substance, an astral brain, the whole mechanism becomes explainable.

Anything Once Known is Never Forgotten.—We know something of the way physical sensations are transmitted to the physical brain, namely, by nerve currents that follow the nerves much as electricity follows a wire. These nerve currents actually are electrical in nature and communicate movements to the brain that result in setting up a state of consciousness.

But such motions in time die away; yet memory shows that in some manner they are preserved. What preserves them, and how? The sensations thus recorded on the physical brain may be entirely forgotten for years—showing that the motions in the physical brain have ceased—and then be suddenly recalled. How does this happen? Or sensations may be completely forgotten by the objective consciousness, and entirely beyond recall by any objective process, yet be recovered when the person is in a state of hypnotic trance.

It is by experiments with subjects under such hypnotic influence that we know nothing felt or known is ever forgotten. What substance is fine and strong enough to preserve the most delicate impressions for an indefinite period? Scarcely the nerve currents, which are constantly changing, rippling along the fine wires of the nerves and hurrying one sensation on top of another as a telephone wire carries the sound of voices. The telephone does not remember; the phonograph, in a way, does. Connect the telephone to a phonographic blank disc and the impressions made are comparatively permanent. What is the phonographic disc attached to the human brain? It is evident that the motions transmitted through the nerves to the brain are retained permanently in some substance which is capable under proper conditions of again imparting them to the brain in something closely resembling their original form and intensity. Whatever this substance may be, it certainly is something not subject to physical or chemical change.

But if we consider that accompanying and interpenetrating the physical brain is an astral brain, composed of frictionless substance with the property of
permanently recording impressions, the matter is
cleared up. As every motion imparted to astral substance is retained indefinitely, every sensation which
imparts motion to the astral brain is registered in a
comparatively ineffaceable manner. It is not retained
by the physical brain, because the physical substance
is constantly removed and replenished, and any
movement in its parts is retarded by friction, even
its molecular motion, which expresses as heat, being
subject to retardation through cooling. But even as
space offers imperceptible resistance to rays of light,
or to the planetary bodies passing through it, so
astral substance retains permanently, or practically
so, all motions imparted to it. Under proper conditions these motions residing in the astral brain can
be focused on the electromagnetism of the physical
brain and impart motions to it in such a manner that
it is recognized objectively; and the resultant consciousness is then called memory.

The astral brain in which memory resides is commonly called the Subjective Mind, the Subliminal
Mind, the Subconscious Mind, or the Unconscious
Mind. The better and more recent works on psychology call it the Unconscious Mind. It is constituted of those motions derived from experience that
reside—organized in a manner later to be explained
—in the astral form and do not at the time transmit
their motions to the physical brain, remaining below
the threshold of objective consciousness; while the

Objective Mind, on the other hand, is constituted of those motions derived from experience that reside in the astral form which at the time are able to communicate their energies to electromagnetism in sufficient power to transmit their motions to the physical brain and thus impress Objective Consciousness.

As an iceberg largely remains submerged below the surface of the sea, so man has one mind, or soul, but the major portion of it, the unconscious mind, remains below the surface of objective consciousness. It is only that small, keen, bright clever reasoning peak of his mind, or soul, which emerges above the surface of objective consciousness which is designated as the objective mind.

Psychologists recognize that comparatively few of the actions of man or of other forms of life result from the direction of the objective mind. Many of the physiological processes, for instance, such as assimilation, secretion and circulation, are carried on during sleep. They are wholly directed by the unconscious mind. And the unconscious mind in turn is influenced about equally by the physical environment and the astral environment.

Man is About Equally Influenced by Two Environments.—Man has a physical body, and he has an astral body. The physical body, and through its nerve currents, which are electrical in nature, his mind, or soul, which resides on the inner plane—the small emergent part being the Objective Mind and the submerged part the Unconscious Mind—are influenced by his outer-plane environment. His astral body and his mind, or soul, are influenced by his inner-plane environment; and the thought-cells so affected in turn influence his physical body. Thus does man live in, and is influenced by, both an outer-plane world and an inner-plane world.

From the outer world he is influenced by the objects and people he contacts, by what people say— either vocally or through screen portrayal or the printed page—and by the weather. Objects and people also influence him from the inner plane, but instead of through physical contact chiefly through their character vibrations. From the inner plane he is also influenced, not by what people say, but by their thoughts and the thoughts of other life-forms. From the inner plane he is also influenced by the weather; but this weather is not physical, it is the impact of astrological energies.

As to the degree in which man while still on earth is influenced by each of his two environments, there has been a vast amount of observation, carefully checked, which indicates that if we consider man to consist of his physical body, his astral body, his mind, or soul, and the thoughts he thinks, the inner-plane environment—which includes objects, the actions and thoughts of intelligent entities, and astrological energies—has as much influence over his thoughts, feelings and behavior as do all outer-plane conditions and energies, including the influence of his associates.

This being true, it behooves people to gain as much knowledge as possible about their inner-plane environment in addition to knowledge of the outer-plane environment. While they usually think of it in different terms, almost everyone realizes that his survival depends upon his ability to adapt himself to his environment, and that the more perfectly he adapts himself to his environment the more successful he becomes. His ability to adapt himself to his environment depends upon his knowledge of himself and that environment and the extent to which he makes application of that knowledge. Consequently, the individual ignorant of the astral world and its energies can live only half as successfully as if he understood and used knowledge of both planes.

Inner-Plane Senses.—Relative to physical sensations, biologists hold that at first there was only one diffused primal sensitivity or irritibility in response to stimulus. It is assumed that this diffused primal sensitivity was the sense of touch. In ameboid life, for instance, it is assumed that there is only the world of tangible objects accessible through actual physical contact which is apprehended through the sense of touch and possibly a rudimentary sense of temperature. Then as evolution took place, through a vast amount of trial and error, the other senses slowly and gradually developed from this sense of touch. Taste is one specialization of this sense of touch. Smell is the sense of touch developed in a slightly different direction so that things can be touched a bit more remotely. Another canalization of this sense of touch is the ability to apprehend and interpret vibrations of air by the faculty of hearing.

It is common also to include the sense of sight as

one of the five physical senses. It is the ability to sense and interpret waves of energy called light. But as light is not material, strictly speaking the ability to reach out, not merely feet or miles as with the sense of hearing, but also across light-years of empty space, as we do with sight, is hardly physical unless we interpret all common perception as physical. In that case, because animals commonly apprehend conditions through intuition, and telepathy is a common means of communication among them, we are justified in adopting the classification of the ancients and considering all seven as physical senses.

As already mentioned, university experiments have proved the existence also of an inner-plane faculty of apprehending information. It is called the faculty of extra-sensory perception. It embraces all inner-plane means of gaining information. And undoubtedly animals other than man possess this faculty in some degree.

But even as the diffused primal sense of touch became canalized and specialized, so extra-sensory perception by which the unconscious mind of creatures apprehends things on the inner plane, through exercise and effort at discrimination becomes specialized and more serviceable. We may assume that this sensitivity to inner-plane entities and their vibrations, to the thoughts of intelligent entities, and to astrological energies is universal in some degree with lifeforms. But ability in selection and interpretation of inner-plane conditions by this universal sense varies widely.

An artist may take his dog to an art gallery. If it happens to be a greyhound, it has keener sight than its master. The dog can see all the pictures in the gallery as easily as can the artist. But the effect upon his consciousness is vastly different. The dog simply sees flat surfaces daubed with color. If a bone is pictured, he pays no attention to it. He has neither the power to select a picture which conveys information or emotional appeal, nor the power to give it interpretation.

Nor is it because they cannot look about them on the inner plane with the senses of the astral form that people fail to gain more information through extra-sensory perception. In some degree at least all people have the faculty of extra-sensory perception. But more often than not they cannot focus the attention of their unconscious mind on the information sought, and even when they do they often are unable to interpret it correctly. And in addition—the most formidable barrier of all—when their unconscious mind perceives something important correctly, it is unable to compete with cerebral activity and sense impressions which monopolize the electrical energies of the brain and nervous system which must be used to impress a thought or sensation on the brain and thus bring it into objective consciousness.

Even as on the physical plane the general sense of touch has been specialized into different types of perception, so also on the inner plane the general extra-sensory faculty has been specialized. Corresponding to touch is the astral sense of psychometry. Corresponding to taste is the astral sense of energy absorption. Corresponding to smell is the astral sense of aroma detection. Corresponding to hearing is the astral sense of clairaudience. Corresponding to sight is the astral sense of clairvoyance. Corresponding to intuition is the astral faculty of inspiration. Corresponding to telepathy is the astral faculty of spiritual communion.

On the inner plane all things and thoughts in the universe seem to be related to each other in precisely the same manner that all experiences and thoughts which the individual has ever had persist and are related to each other in his own unconscious mind. And for the individual to contact those he desires to contact with the appropriate astral sense and bring them before the attention of objective consciousness the same laws are operative and must be used that enable him to contact and bring to the attention of objective consciousness the memory of thoughts and experiences he has forgotten.

In Course V, Esoteric Psychology, it is pointed out that all mental processes are governed by the LAW OF ASSOCIATION. Among the most powerful associations by Resemblance is that of identical or similar resonance. This is the key to making contact with things or thoughts, past, present or future, on the inner plane; for there thoughts and things having the same vibration are together. Distance on the inner plane is of a different order than in the physical world; there it is measured by disparity in vibratory rates.

On the physical plane the visibility of things and the audibility of sounds diminish with distance, and thus the number of objects it is possible to see or the sounds that can be heard is narrowly limited. But virtually all experimenters in ESP are agreed that distance has no effect on extra-sensory perception. That which is on the other side of the earth is as easily seen as that which is in the same room, and the thought of a person on the other side of the earth is as easily apprehended as the thought of a person in the same room. If the pronouncements of university scientists who have experimented exhaustively with extra-sensory perception are to be taken seriously, nothing in the universe is beyond the range of extra-sensory perception, and thus the number of things which it is possible to see clairvoyantly is infinite.

Furthermore, on the inner plane time is of a different order, and consciousness can direct its attention either forward or backward and by means of the appropriate astral sense perceive objects, life-forms and thoughts as they existed in the past or as they will exist in the future.

These are the potentialities of the astral senses; potentialities meagerly employed as yet by man on earth. But for that matter man has only recently begun to utilize the potentialities of his own outer-plane senses and reason. Potentially they make accessible incalculable knowledge of physics, chemistry and electricity; yet it is only in late years we have used them to acquire that knowledge on which is founded modern science and industry.

Most people, however, at some time in their lives, have observed authentic instances of the operation of one of the astral senses. Spontaneous information has come to them, or to one of their acquaintances, in a manner that precludes its acquisition through reason and the outer-plane senses. And there are others, usually unaware of the source or manner of their inspiration, who employ their astral senses in making contact with information on the inner plane, and bring this information up into objective consciousness in the course of their creative work. These are the people to whom we apply the title genius.

All genius draws upon information acquired by its unconscious mind which is less accessible to the objective minds of others. Whether it is the great poet, the great artist, the musical prodigy, the mathematical wizard or the most outstanding personalities in science and invention, they each and all, as their biographies reveal, either in dreams, in states of exhaustion resulting from concentration on their problems, while in semi-reverie, or other states which favor the unconscious impressing the information it has gained on the brain, have experienced uprushes from the unconscious mind which have given them knowledge or ability beyond that of those to whom the term genius cannot be applied.

While those who train their psychic faculties, and those who have outstanding spontaneous extra-sensory experiences, usually know the information is coming through from the inner plane, most people are unable to distinguish between their normal thoughts and opinions and those derived from extra-sensory sources. In the university experiments it is reported that those who give good performances are unable to determine at the time whether extra-sensory perception is operating and therefore whether or not what they are doing is directed by anything but chance. Even of those who employ extra-sensory perception most successfully, it is only the rare individual who can be sure when he is or is not using it.

But merely the ability to employ the astral senses does not confer genius. Genius must have a brain which can, and does, utilize the information and power which uprushes from the unconscious. It requires the harmonious co-operation of the Unconscious Mind and the Objective Mind.

Personal Survival After Death.—As demonstrated under hypnosis and in psychoanalysis, nothing known by the individual is ever forgotten. His experiences, including his thoughts and the expression of personal traits, are organized and retained in frictionless astral substance. That this inner-plane organization, which expresses as an identifiable personality, survives beyond the tomb is attested by a vast and steadily increasing mass of evidence, as set forth in the writings of Dr. John King, Sir Oliver Lodge, Sir Arthur Conan Doyle, Rev. G. Vale Owen, J. Arthur Hill, Horace Leaf, Ella Wheeler Wilcox, W. T. Stead, Dr. A. D. Watson, William O. Stevens, Stewart Edward White, and a score of others.

Those who have passed to the inner plane may,

or may not, have acquired information of value. In psychic work, when information comes through in a continuous stream of intelligence, one may be sure it is coming from some inner-plane entity. It is the opinion of this inner-plane entity which is being received. When information arrives in messages which are continuous, they are not merely the conclusions of the individual himself derived from his own inner-plane observations. Conclusions reached by the unconscious from its own inner-plane observations, and information acquired through the independent use of its astral senses, do not come through as a continuous stream of intelligence, or a well formulated message, but as uprushes from the unconscious, as flash after flash of relevant information, which only when pieced together gives complete knowledge of the matter about which knowledge is sought.

ASTRAL VIBRATIONS

Serial No. 41

THE CHURCH OF LIGHT
Box 1525, Los Angeles 53, California

Printed in U.S.A.

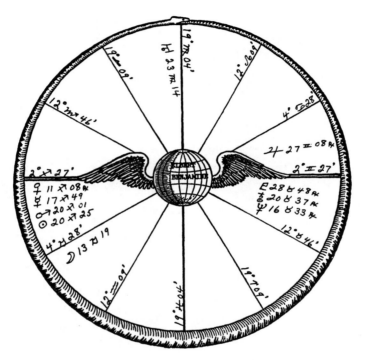

ELBERT BENJAMINE (C. C. ZAIN), Dec. 12, 1882, 5:55 a.m. 94W. 41—39N.

1898 (autumn), began occult studies, Mercury conjunction Moon r, Mercury sesqui-square Pluto p.

1900, contacted The Brotherhood of Light and commenced serious study of astrology, Mercury trine Neptune r.

1910 (spring), gave promise to write the 21 Courses of B. of L. lessons, Sun semi-sextile Mercury r.

1914, March 21, started work on lessons, Mercury sesqui-square Jupiter p, Mercury sesqui-square Uranus r.

1915, May, started B. of L. in Los Angeles, and classes that still continue without interruption, Sun trine Uranus r.

1934, Feb. 20, finished writing the 21 Courses of B. of L. lessons, Mars trine Pluto r, Mercury trine Jupiter p.

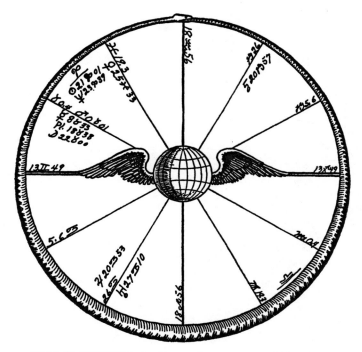

FRED H. SKINNER, April 10, 1872, 8:09 a.m. 93W. 41N.

1909 (Nov. 14), started studying astrology, Sun sextile Uranus *r* in 3rd.

1917, resigned from secret occult society, Venus, ruler of 12th, trine Saturn *r*, sextile Jupiter *r*.

1918 (autumn), joined B. of L., Sun P Jupiter *p*, Venus conjunction Moon *r*. Started teaching astrology, Sun sesqui-square Saturn *r*, ruler of 9th.

1919 (autumn) started teaching B. of L. classes and continued teaching without interruption until his death in 1940, Jupiter conjunction Uranus *r*, Venus semi-sextile Neptune *r*.

1932 (autumn), vice-president of The Church of Light, Sun semi-sextile Pluto *p*.

1934, started issuing questionnaires for use of C. of L. teachers, Sun inconjunct Saturn *r*, semi-sextile Jupiter *r*.

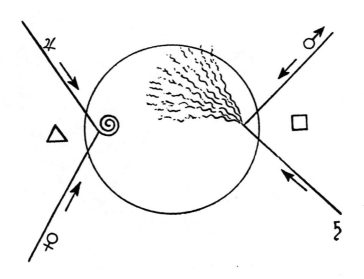

ASTRAL VIBRATIONS

I T is common knowledge that the energy of all life on earth is transmitted across space from the sun. Furthermore, we are also taught that all physical bodies exert a gravitational influence upon all other physical bodies independent of whether or not there are other physical bodies between them. Then again, energy is propelled to far distant points by radio. Yet in spite of the general recognition of these facts the great scientific men of the world are quite unagreed as to the nature of light, gravitation and radio. How then am I to explain still another form of energy which, like that commonly recognized as coming from the sun, has a wide variety of influences, like gravitation is unhampered by passing through obstacles, and like radio is capable of conveying intelligence? Such a form of energy is astral vibration.

Not so long ago scientific men were agreed that light is the ether moving in transverse waves. But even as the chemistry of the nineteenth century has been displaced by entirely new conceptions, so we find physics and mechanics and geometry also in the throes of revolution. This started with the apparent verification of Einstein's Theory of Relativity by the eclipse observations of May 29, 1919, and September 21, 1921. And it has been gaining momentum since through this theory's apparent verification by all the experiments that thus far have been devised to test its validity.

It may be pointed out that the test of any theory is its ability to predict new phenomena and to correct all known phenomena in the field which it covers. Einstein's Special Theory of Relativity may ultimately fall, just as the recently accepted theories of chemistry, those of geometry, those even of mechanics, as well as those of biology have fallen in the face of new discoveries. But at the present moment Einstein's Special Theory meets the above mentioned tests better than any other advanced in the realms of mathematics and physics. And in the same manner the theory of astral substance and astral vibration covers the field of biology, astrology and psychic phenomena better than any yet set forth. No other theory has been forthcoming satisfactorily to explain a mass of carefully collected astrological, biological and psychological facts.

The theory of astral substance and astral vibration, however, does adequately explain all the known facts of astrology, of psychic phenomena, of biology and of psychology. And at the same time in each of the sciences mentioned it has been able to predict new phenomena, such as, for instance, the influence of certain positions of Uranus, Neptune and Pluto upon life before such positions had ever actually been observed, and the possibilities and apparent limitations of divination.

But it is not to be supposed that the theory of astral substance and astral vibration as here set forth may not in time need considerable revision to keep pace with new conceptions, such as that suggested in the final paragraph of Chapter III of The Evolution of Physics (1938), by Albert Einstein and Leopold Infeld; "The theory of relativity stresses the importance of the field concept in physics. But we have not yet succeeded in formulating a pure field physics. For the present we must still assume the existence of both: field and matter." And while the astral field concept may take precedence in the future, for the present we must continue to speak both of astral substance and astral vibrations.

This pure field concept relates to Einstein's General Theory. The Special Theory of Relativity, which is now taught in most universities as fundamental to understanding physics does not make it a necessity. And as we will have repeated occasions to refer to this Special Theory of Relativity, its present standing in university circles should be established. For this purpose let me quote from an article by H. P. Robertson, Ph.D., Professor of Mathematical Physics, Princeton University, which appeared in the June, 1939, issue of Scientific American Magazine:

"In view of these developments one may say that at present the special theory of relativity is one of the most thoroughly accepted and most firmly established doctrines of modern physics. It has permeated the field of mechanics, electromagnetism (including optics) and atomic physics; while it may appear desirable to have further direct checks on the validity of its mechanical aspects, a deviation from the predicted effects would constitute a most puzzling—and, at least temporarily distressing—jolt for modern physics."

This Special Theory of Relativity holds that physical velocities cannot exceed that of light, and that anything moving with a velocity of light no longer possesses length, has infinite mass and so is practically impervious to the pull of gravitation, and that for it time has come to a standstill.

According to Einstein, if a bullet could be shot from a gun with a velocity of 160,000 miles per second, due to its motion the bullet would shrink to about half its previous length. Yes, and we may add that if the same bullet could be shot from a gun with a velocity greater than light it would not only lose its length, but its other physical properties, and then exist as a bullet on the astral plane. Einstein's assertion that nothing can move faster than light is true of physical things. But to cover all phases of existence it must be modified by the explanation that anything that moves faster than light is no longer physical, and therefore is not a thing according to Einstein's conception—for it then loses all its physical properties and acquires those of the astral world.

The reason that light, radio and other electromagnetic phenomena present so many difficulties in the way of explaining their behavior, is that they have velocities intermediate between those of slow-moving physical substance and fast-moving astral substance. And it is because the gap between the velocity of physical substance and the velocity of astral substance is too great to bridge, that the inner-plane world affects the outer-plane world, and the outer-plane world affects the inner-plane world only through first imparting motion to electromagnetic energy which has a velocity intermediate and thus can be directly influenced by, and directly influence, both the low-velocity and the high-velocity regions.

But when we speak of velocities, we must not confuse these with frequency of vibration; although when vibratory frequencies of low-velocity physical substance become high enough they are able to influence electromagnetic energies, and when electromagnetic energies have certain frequencies they are able to influence the high-velocity astral world.

Vibratory frequencies of from about 16 per second to 30,000 per second—about 12 octaves—in physical substance can be distinguished by the human ear as sound. Death-dealing vibrations in physical substances of frequencies higher than those commonly employed in radio have been developed in laboratories; but they cannot be heard.

Those used in radio are not vibrations of physical substance. They are electromagnetic frequencies. Such as are used in commercial radio have frequencies of from 550,000 to 1,600,000 per second. The short and the ultra-short radio waves have frequencies considerably higher. But these Hertzian radiations are only the lower electromagnetic frequencies. Above them are the infra-red, or dark-heat waves. Light, which is about 45 octaves above sound, and is electromagnetic rather than physical, is next above the infra-red. We can feel the sensation of heat for about two octaves and see the vibrations as light only for about one octave. Above visible light is ultra-violet radiation, which is sometimes called the chemical ray. Of higher frequency still are the X-rays, and the gamma rays are still higher. As all of these are vibrations in the Boundary-Line realm of velocities, they are referred to as different bands in the electromagnetic spectrum.

Now under certain conditions physical substance gains the power profoundly to influence electromagnetic energies: and under certain conditions electromagnetic energies gain the power profoundly to influence astral substance. For instance, when an iron is heated its molecules are given greater speed. They are physical substance. But when they attain a certain frequency of oscillation the iron becomes red hot or white hot and then radiates light, which is not physical, but an electromagnetic radiation.

A current of electricity moving over a wire develops a field of force about the wire. If it is an alternating current of low frequency, say of 60 cycles such as is commonly used in transmitting electricity for light and power, at each reversal practically all of the field of energy folds back on the wire. But under certain conditions the energy does not mostly fold back, but keeps right on going. The conditions are that the oscillations must be sufficiently frequent. When they attain sufficient frequency the energy radiates, and we have waves such as are used in radio.

Furthermore, even as molecular vibrations, which are physical, when they attain certain frequencies are able to impart much energy to electromagnetic waves; and electrical energies, which are at least granular, moving over wires when given certain frequencies radiate non-physical energy into space; so electromagnetic energies generated in living organisms when given certain frequencies are able profoundly to affect energies of the still higher-velocity astral world.

And when astral-world velocities are attained, existence acquires properties that are contradictory to physical experience, but which are none the less consistent with what the Special Theory of Relativity demands when such velocities are present. Under these velocities time as we know it no longer exists, distance as we know it disappears and is supplanted by difference in vibratory frequency, gravitation gives way and its place is taken by the principle of resonance, and instead of mechanical power thought-energy performs many similar functions. These new properties of existence, displacing those with which we are so familiar on the physical plane, permit of various conditions that contradict material experience.

Now all of this, I am well aware, may seem to some highly technical. But it is a necessary prelude, in view of latest scientific opinion, to any adequate discussion of astral vibration. And it leads up to a consideration of astrology.

It may be thought that in the third lesson of a course designed to lead the student by easy and systematic steps from complete ignorance of such sub-

jects to a grasp of those fundamental principles which
it is advisable to know before attempting the detailed
mastery of the various occult sciences, that the subject of astrology is out of place. This is not the case,
however, and the student will find that the sooner he
grasps the general significance of astrology the quick-
er and the easier will he be able to master the whole
range of the occult.

This is true for two distinct reasons. One is that
all life is constantly being influenced by unseen currents of energy radiated by the planets. Consequently, the precise effect of any other occult force at any
given time cannot be known unless the power of
planetary currents to modify its influence also be
taken into account.

The other reason is that through a peculiar sympathy that pervades all Nature, and the fact that
Nature tends to express similar qualities in numerous
octaves, when the planetary affinity of an object is
known—it being but the expression of the same quality on one octave that the planet expresses on another
octave of Nature's scale—this planetary rulership, as
it is called, affords a true index to otherwise unknown
attributes of the object. Thus through their relationship to the orbs above we easily learn the occult properties of things we otherwise might never know.
Astrology, therefore, is the golden key that unlocks
the mysteries. It is the most perfect instrument in
existence, I am convinced, for the interpretation of
man's true relation to the universe and to God. And
as a religion is what man believes to be his relation
to the universe and to God, when rightly understood,

there can be no more perfect religion than the Religion of the Stars.

Now right here is where the student proves himself liberal-minded or a bigot. He may recoil upon his egotism and declare he knows he has a free-will and that the stars have no power to influence him. Yet while agreeing with him in the matter of free will, for astrology does not imply fatality, I must point out that the question of whether he is influenced by streams of energy from the planets impinging upon his astral body can be decided, as can any scientific fact, only by experimental evidence.

In spite of educational prejudice, or preconception, if he will put his opinions to the test, and before passing final judgment learn to erect a chart and judge it according to the rules of the science, he will then indicate a true scientific spirit. But many are afraid to put their ideas to the test. They are so self-opinionated they will not investigate anything with which they are not already familiar. They pass sentence without trial, preferring to remain in the rut of error rather than take the trouble to determine the correctness of their opinions. Such an attitude is inexcusable and leads to stagnation. To condemn a subject without examination is bigotry. And such bigotry is equaled in its folly only by many prevalent mystical notions that anyone of average intelligence who takes the pains to investigate carefully can quickly and completely disprove.

If it apparently does not seem reasonable that streams of unseen energy radiated by the planets af-

fect human life and destiny, let us consider that
listening to an opera by radio also seems unreasonable. To be sure, nothing seems more unreasonable
than life itself; and scientists have puzzled over it
centuries without offering any adequate explanation
of it. Yet it exists. And the only way to determine if
the planets influence human life is to experiment with
them. Any person of average intelligence can in a
short time, and at trifling expense for tables of the
positions of the planets—those for one year being
called an Ephemeris—for various years, learn to set
up a map showing the positions of the planets at the
time of birth of each of his friends and relatives.
Such a map is called a horoscope. From examining
such charts it will be apparent very shortly that persons born near noon, when the sun is overhead, have
great ambition and ultimately rise to a position of
prominence in the particular environment in which
they move. It will quickly be recognized that persons born just before sunrise also have a power to
rise in the world, in these cases through personal
effort, and they continue the struggle to rise as long
as life lasts. Then the next step in the investigation
will be convincing that any person born when the
plant Mars is rising on the eastern horizon is aggressive and warlike; but if Saturn is there instead, the
person is careful and cautious.

Still more advanced experiments, in which the
movements of the planets after birth are calculated,
will show that special after-birth positions, called
progressed aspects, coincide with specific events in
the life, and that from progressed aspects the time

and characteristics of events can, within rather narrow limits, be predicted. This is not fatality, it is merely the ability to predict by astronomical calculations when certain streams of energy will fall upon the person's astral body in such a way as to give unusual activity to certain thought-cells within the person's unconscious mind. The person, if aware of the currents reaching him from the planets, does not need to act in the manner usually indicated. But if unaware of the influence, the thought-cells thus stimulated lead him to fulfill the prediction.

Someone may now interpose the objection that astrologers still use the geocentric positions of the planets, but that astronomers have long ago abandoned geocentric astronomy. This is a misconception, for every astrologer knows that the sun is the center of the Solar System. So does the astronomer, yet when he wishes to calculate where the shadow of an eclipse will fall upon the earth, or when he wishes to determine the moment a star will cross the meridian, he does not calculate these positions in reference to the sun as a center, but in reference to some particular point on the earth. Likewise the mariner does not calculate the position of a star with reference to the sun as a center to find his position at sea. He must know the position of the star in relation to the earth, and to some definite spot on the earth, at some particular interval of time.

So even as the light of the star that enables the mariner to find his position at sea comes to the earth from a given angle at a given time, making his cal-

culations possible, likewise the energies from the
planets that influence life reach the earth from given
directions at given times. And it is the direction from
which these energies are received on the earth, and
the manner in which they converge and combine on
earth, that determines their influence upon earthly
life and destiny.

It is true that astrologers sometimes fail in their
predictions; but when the published report of one of
the largest and best equipped hospitals in the land
shows that in diagnosing disease 53 per cent of its
diagnoses, as shown by hospital records, have been
wrong, we should be somewhat lenient with astrologers. ("Dr. Richard Cabot says of the findings of
the Massachusetts General Hospital Clinic, where
precision is carried to the nth degree, that post mor-
tem examination proves that in forty-seven per cent
the diagnosis of the clinic is correct." — William
Howard Hay, M.D., in Progress, for September,
1923.)

Architects also make blunders at times, and chemists sometimes fail in their analyses and in their syn-
thetic processes. Even astronomers occasionally err
in their calculations. The fault in each of these cases
is not so much the fault of the science as the fallibility
of those employing it. None of the sciences is yet
in a perfected state, but with the same amount of
critical investigation astrology will rival, I am per-
suaded, other sciences in the precision of its results.

Nature of Planetary Influences.—Having, I hope,
made it plain that the rules of astrological practice

are independent of any theory, and that their accuracy should be determined by observation, let us next inquire into the probable manner in which planetary positions indicate the character at birth, and afterward by giving new energy to certain thought-cells, have an influence over the life.

To start with, we know that the sun is a giant electromagnet radiating lines of energy into space, and that these lines of energy are cut by the various planets revolving around the sun much as the armatures of a dynamo, as commonly installed in our power plants, cut the lines of energy radiated by the electromagnet at the center. I quote from an article by Edgar Lucian Larkin, director of Mt. Lowe Observatory, published in the spring of 1923:

"The astronomers at the Mt. Wilson Observatory made a great discovery with their new delicate magnetometers, that rotating sun spots are surrounded by an electromagnetic field of force, and magnetic lines extend to space. This is an important fact in Nature. A dynamo is a rotating metallic mass in an electromagnetic field of force between poles. Then the earth is an armature, since it contains metals and is in rapid rotation."

The great physicist, Tyndall, many years ago indicated how dependent upon the sun are most mechanical actions, chemical changes, and other manifestations of power on the surface of the earth. And to this conception, investigators into the occult have added the assurance that whatever of a mental and spiritual nature is expressed on earth also derives its energy from the sun.

The sun, then, should be regarded as sending forth not only light, radiant heat, electromagnetic energy, and exerting the power of gravitation, but also as radiating still finer energies through astral and spiritual substances which when expressed manifest as mental and moral attributes. In fact, whatever energies exist upon the earth, we may be sure they were chiefly derived from the sun.

The boundless regions of space undoubtedly are fields of energy; for thousands of universes other than our own, with all its countless hordes of suns and systems, are known to be rushing through it with an average speed, so astronomers say, of 480 miles per second. These universes, over a million of which are known to exist, have long been recognized as Spiral Nebulae, and they certainly radiate energies other than the light by which they are seen. Our universe, known as the Galaxy, or Milky Way, also is traveling at a distance of 100,000 to 1,000,000 light-years from the other known universes. (Light travels 186,284 miles per second, according to 1942 findings, and one light-year is the distance light travels in one year.) And while there are stars in our universe that move with much greater speed, and some that move slower, the more than a billion suns comprising our universe have a usual speed among themselves of from 8 to 21 miles per second. Our sun, carrying with it the earth and other planets of the Solar System, travels with a speed of about $12\frac{1}{2}$ miles per second; and the earth on which we live moves in its orbit around the sun at the rate of $18\frac{1}{2}$ miles per second. These figures, of course, stagger the imagination. But I have taken them from the recent reports of well recognized astronomers for the purpose of indicating that the heavenly bodies are moving with great speed, and that, as we know through the very fact of being able to see them, they are each radiating energy. Therefore, as they move, each in its appointed path, they cut fields of energy set up by the other moving suns and universes.

This being the case we may regard our sun as a great step-down transformer. Our earth and the other planets probably are not suitably constituted for handling the high frequencies that abound in the path of the sun. We are most of us aware that the voltage of electricity as it comes from a power-house to be carried any distance is too high to be used in the ordinary electric appliances. It is necessary to install transformers to lower the voltage before the current is permitted to flow over the lighting system or common power wires. So the sun may be looked upon, not merely as a dynamo, but as a transformer of the high-tension energies of space, stepping them down to such frequencies that they set up a new field of energy about the sun.

The planets revolving about the Sun in elliptical paths cut the energy field of the sun. This is not an electromagnetic field of energy only, but also an astral energy field and a spiritual energy field. And the planets cutting this huge energy field in turn become transformers and transmitters of energy. That is, each being of different chemical composition and different density of material, they each are adapted to picking up energies and stepping them down to certain other frequencies and radiating these into space.

In this manner, similar in principle to that which may be observed in modern electrical appliances, the energies of space are gathered up by the sun and again radiated. Then the planets gather up this energy, and each giving it a special trend, again radiate it into space. Thus it reaches the earth and man from the particular direction occupied by the planets at the time, and endowed with the particular attributes imparted to it by each.

As no one up to the present time has been able to explain in a thoroughly satisfactory manner just what light, magnetism and electricity are, it would be premature for me to try to explain just what the astral light is. But this energy by which the influence of the planets is transmitted to the earth is seen by clairvoyants as a peculiar light. It varies in color and luminosity even as the sunlight does, and seems to be the all-pervading medium of vision for those who have left the physical plane and now live in the adjacent astral realms.

As physical science is in heated debate as to how light and other electromagnetic energies traverse space, we need not be too positive as to the nature of the vibrations that transmit energy from the planets to the astral body of man and other things; but we need not remain in doubt that such energies do reach and influence all things upon the earth. For this is a matter easily ascertained by experiment.

Then again, if I am asked why planetary influence is ranged so that there are seven distinct kinds of influence, one kind being transmitted by each of the seven planets more anciently known, and the more recently discovered planets Uranus, Neptune and Pluto transmitting an influence that is the octave expression of Mercury, Venus and the Moon, I can only answer it is because the septenary division is the one mostly adhered to by Nature. Why is it there are seven tones in music, the eighth being a higher expression of the first? Why does the light that comes from the sun, when passed through a prism, or as seen in a rainbow, dissolve itself into seven distinct colors? Why is it that the 92 chemical elements also tend to follow the same septenary law, the atomic number being determined by the number of electrons revolving about the nucleus of an atom, given multiples of such electrons expressing similar qualities on lower and higher octaves, as witnessed in bromine, iodine, chlorine and fluorine, which each express qualities common to all, but with greater or less activity? The impulses and thoughts of man, likewise, are susceptible to a grouping in which there are seven well marked families, and in which three of the families have expressions on a higher octave which gives them additional characteristics.

Therefore, even as in other departments of Nature, so we observe in planetary influences also, a definite grouping of qualities. We find the same quality that is expressed by the influence of a planet upon human life to be expressed in sound by a certain musical tone, to be expressed in color by a certain hue, to be expressed among minerals by a certain metal, to be expressed among stones by a certain gem, to be expressed among numbers and letters by certain of each, to be expressed among human thoughts by a definite group, and among peoples by particular nations. In other words, the same quality of energy expresses in all these and many other domains of existence, but in each case the expression belongs to a given octave.

1. The Sun, as directly affecting life upon the earth, radiates those frequencies of astral light that produce a dignified and lifegiving influence. It is the same quality that expresses in terms of ordinary light as the color Orange. It expresses in sound as the tone D, and in human thought as Power.

2. The Moon, cutting the field of energy set up by the sun, and the field also due to the earth, is so composed that the wave-lengths and frequencies it transmits into space exert an influence that is plastic and receptive. It is the same quality that expresses in terms of color as the Green ray of the solar spectrum. It expresses in sound as the tone F, and in human thought as Domesticity.

3. The planet Mercury, acting as a transformer and transmitter of energy, radiates an influence that is sharp, active, changeable and clever. It is the same quality that expresses in color as Violet. It expresses in sound as the tone B, and in human thought as Intelligence.

4. Venus transforms the solar energies to a different rate of vibration. Her influence is clinging

and submissive. It is the love quality which expresses in color as the Yellow ray. In sound it expresses as the tone E, and in human thought as Sociability.

5. The energies radiated by the sun when gathered up and transformed to a different rate by the planet Mars exert an influence energetic and combative. It is the same quality that expresses in color as Red. In sound it is the tone C, and in human thought Aggression.

6. Jupiter, largest of all the planets, transmits an influence that is cheerful and beneficent. It is the same quality that expresses in color as the Indigo ray of the solar spectrum. It expresses in sound as the tone A, and in human thought as Religion.

7. Saturn, the planet with the ring around it, transforms the energies it receives into such wavelengths and frequencies that they exert an influence that is cold and reflective. It is the same quality that expresses in color as Blue. In sound it expresses as the tone G, and in human thought as Safety.

8. Uranus is merely the higher octave of Mercury, transmitting an influence original and disruptive. It is a quality expressed in color by all combined into a dazzling white. Its tones are above the physical, such as the astral chimes often heard by psychics. It expresses in human thought as Individuality.

9. Neptune is the octave of Venus, and transmits an influence visionary and idealistic. It is a quality expressed by irridescence, in which colors glint and change and flow one into another. Its tones are like-

wise above the physical, combining as the music of the spheres, and in human thought the same quality expresses as the Utopian.

10.   Pluto is the octave of the Moon, transmitting an influence that is forceful and compelling. The domestic impulses are expanded to embrace a larger group. It is a quality expressed by ultra-violet or infra-red in color, and by either harmony or discord of tones. In human thought it expresses as Universal Welfare.

Signs Act As Sounding Boards.—As an instrument affects the tone sounded on it, it should also be expected that the tone quality of a given planetary influence is greatly affected by the astral conditions of the particular portion of the heavens occupied by the planet at the time the note is sounded. We are well aware, for instance, that the effect upon the ear of the tone C is much different when the tone emanates from a cello than when it emanates from a calliope.

Due to the field of energy of the combined sun and earth the astral vibrations received from the planets when in one part of the heavens and those received when in a different part of the heavens, although always the same in pitch, are different in tone quality. That is, they are sent from various sounding boards. Observation proves that the path in which the sun and planets apparently move about the earth is divided into twelve distinct sounding boards, or instruments, for astral tones. This path in which the sun and planets apparently travel is called the Zodiac. It commences, due to the polarity of the earth in relation to the sun, at that portion of the sky where the sun crosses the celestial equator from the south to the north in spring each year. The north and south hemispheres of the earth, as indicated by the magnetic needle, are of opposite polarity, and where the sun apparently crosses from one polarity of the earth to the other in coming north is where the zodiac begins.

This zodiac is divided into twelve equal sections, called signs of the zodiac. Each sign, or section, of the zodiac is named after a particular constellation of stars which pictures its influence, but which does not coincide with it either in location or extent. As each sign of the zodiac has its own quality as a sounding board from which planetary tones may be sent to earth, it follows that the influence of a planet when in one zodiacal sign is not the same as when in another zodiacal sign. The planet Mars, for instance, when in the sign Aries has a pleasing quality like the tone C sounded on a cornet, but when in the sign Cancer the same tone is displeasing like the tone C sounded on an old tin can. This tone quality as influencing life on earth has been determined by careful observation for each planet when in each sign.

Houses Influence Volume and Show Department of Life Affected.—But besides the quality of a tone we must also take into consideration the acoustic conditions where the tone is heard. Due to these conditions, in some great auditoriums it is easy for the slightest tone to be distinctly heard, and in other halls a tone does not carry, or is reflected from walls

and ceilings in such manner as to produce a confusion
of sounds. Of this public speakers are well aware.
And in like manner the astral vibrations reaching any
particular point on the earth are subject to the conditions of the environment in which they are received.
The earth and its atmosphere have an astral counterpart, through which astral vibrations must make
their way to reach any point on the earth's surface.
When these rays come from directly overhead they
have less astral substance to traverse, and when they
come from other directions they have more in varying degree. The surface of the earth, too, is rotating
at the equator at the rate of over one thousand miles
an hour, which evidently has an influence upon the
field of energy about the earth, which again must
have an influence upon any astral waves reaching the
earth's surface at a given point.

So we find that the direction from which the astral
vibrations of the planets are received, with regard to
that point on the earth where received, has an influence upon both the volume and the trend of their
influence. This variation in the volume of a planet's
energy that actually reaches the spot, and the particular trend that is given to it, may be accurately
mapped by a circle divided into twelve equal sections
called Mundane Houses. The circle represents a line
around the earth to the east with the observer at the
center. A horizontal line across the circle represents
a line passing from the eastern to the western horizon. A vertical line through the circle represents a
line from zenith to nadir. Each of the four quad-
rants thus mapped then may be divided into three

equal sections by other lines radiating from the center. And it is found, and may be experimentally verified, that the volume of energy received from a planet when in the section of the sky mapped by one of these Mundane Houses is not the same, nor has it an influence upon the same department of life, as when received from some section of the sky mapped by a different Mundane House.

Aspects Indicate Fortune or Misfortune.—We now have three different factors under consideration, all pertaining to the manner in which the planets affect life upon the earth: 1. The pitch, or tone, of the astral vibration radiated by a planet. 2. The tone quality, or resonance, given to the astral vibration radiated by a planet by the particular zodiacal sign which acts as a sounding board from which it is sounded. 3. The acoustic condition of the auditorium, the point on earth where the astral vibration has an influence, which determines the volume of energy received, and the particular department of life it most influences. And there is yet another consideration before we have spread before us all the more important factors of astrological influence. 4. The manner in which each tone harmonizes or discords with each and all other tones reaching the same spot.

We are doubtless all familiar with the formation of small whirlpools, so frequently to be seen in large numbers at time of high water in our streams. Currents of water meet at just such angles of convergence that they whirl with the proper velocity to form an independent entity, which endures as such for some period of time amid the boiling, seething flood about it. A funnel-shaped hole in the stream is observed, the waters around it forming a rotating wall. Something has been constructed in the surface of the raging torrent that did not before exist. It has properties quite distinct from any other part of the stream. But currents of water meeting under different conditions, from an angle, let us say, that is more obtuse do not form any such entity. They merely roll and toss and foam, as they tumble along, without forming anything distinct and apart from the general current of the stream.

Those of us who have lived on the desert are also familiar with whirling dust columns. Currents of air meeting at just the proper angle form a rotating air column that sucks up sand and dust, and sometimes larger things, the column of whirling sand reaching from earth to sky, moving off across the desert as an entity possessing properties quite apart from the surrounding atmosphere. There are also stronger winds on the desert that give rise to sand storms, but these have not the properties of the whirling columns. Waterspouts and tornadoes are less familiar to most of us, yet they also present an instructive lesson on how currents of air meeting at the proper angle and velocity become agents of terrific power.

Further, light waves under certain circumstances may be brought together in such a manner as to produce, not more light, but less light. This interference of certain light waves with others gives rise to the dark lines of the spectrum. The waves so combine as to cancel each other's motion.

Now, therefore, with these familiar illustrations of water, air and light currents acquiring distinctive properties due to the manner in which they join, we need not be surprised to learn that astral currents when they converge at certain angles possess distinctive properties.

And even as careful study of water currents indicates the conditions under which whirlpools form, so also careful observation has established the conditions under which the astral currents from the planets meet to acquire certain definite influences. Whirlwinds all do not have the same properties. They vary greatly in height, in area, and in movement. Neither do astral currents when they join in such a manner as to acquire distinctive properties, express always the same characteristics. In fact, there are ten different kinds of astral whirls known, each formed by a distinct angle of meeting, and expressing distinctive characteristics.

These astral whirls are not produced by the meeting of the rays of the planets from all angles. They are formed only when the planetary rays meet at definite angles, which have been learned through observation. When the angle at which the astral vibrations from two planets meet is such as to form a definite condition, comparable to a whirlwind, or to a rapids in a river, or to the undertow on an ocean beach, this angle is called an Aspect.

In all, then, there are ten aspects, or definite angles at which planetary rays meet to exert a definite influence. The disturbance in the astral streams when they meet from certain angles is, like a cyclone, very violent and destructive. When they meet from other angles the result is the formation of energies that tend to bind together and build up the astral organisms that they contact. These energies are such that they may be constructively utilized by the astral forms receiving them. But other energies, formed by astral currents meeting at other angles, exhibit an explosive tendency when contacting astral forms.

Experience teaches that astral currents from the planets meeting at a right angle, one-half a right angle, one and one-half a right angle, and twice a right angle, each has a disintegrative, or destructive, influence. A right angle, of course, is ninety degrees, and the aspect formed by planetary rays meeting at a right angle is called a Square.

When planetary rays meet at an angle of one hundred and twenty degrees the aspect is called a Trine. And experience shows that when planetary rays converge at a trine, one-half a trine, or one-fourth a trine, each aspect having an influence peculiar to itself, the influence is distinctly integrative and constructive.

The other three aspects recognized—when two planets are in the same degree of the zodiac, when two planets are in the same degree of declination, and when two planets are one hundred and fifty degrees apart—do not seem integrative or disintegrative in themselves, but depend for their constructive or destructive attributes upon the tone and quality of the planetary streams they combine.

Now the question arises, why it is that all things in the same vicinity are not affected by the planetary streams of energy that converge there in the same way? Before answering this I will ask counter questions. Why is it that when the tone C is sounded in a room where there is a piano, the C string in the piano responds with a sound, and the other strings remain silent? And why is it, listening to a radio, that it is possible to hear a concert given at a distant place, yet not hear other concerts that are being broadcast from the same place using different frequencies? It is because vibrations strike a sympathetic response from, and thus influence, other things having a similar vibratory key.

The astral body of man, and the astral forms of things, contain centers of energy of the same key as each of the planets. But in one person or thing the center of energy keyed to one planet may be so small in volume as to be capable of almost no response, while the center of energy keyed to another planetary influence may be so large that it is constantly sounding a response to the influence of that planet. All persons and things sound a response, transmitting the influence of all the planets in some small degree. But usually the center of energy that transmits the astral vibration of some one planet is more prominent than the centers of energy that respond to those of the other planets. And when it has been determined which planetary influence the person or thing responds to most strongly, the person or thing is said to be Ruled by that planet.

Diverse Functions of Astral Vibrations.—It will now be seen that astral vibration is the means by which energy is communicated from one astral body to another. By it the clairvoyant sees events happening at a great distance, or in the past or in the future. By it tones are carried to the astral ear, giving rise to clairaudience. Events and environment impress their influence upon the astral forms of all things, and these influences being constantly radiated are carried by them to a sensitive person who thus psychometrizes the object. Thoughts are carried from one part of the universe to another by astral vibration from the living to the dead, and from the dead to the living. Also it is the means by which the planets each send a special grade of energy to the earth; and each reaching the earth from a certain sign of the zodiac possesses a specific tone quality; and reaching the thing or person from a given direction, or mundane house, has a special volume and trend; and converging with other planetary rays at given angles results in a definite constructive or destructive influence. Thus does astral vibration underlie all occult manifestation.

DOCTRINE OF NATIVITIES

Serial No. 42

THE CHURCH OF LIGHT
Box 1525, Los Angeles 53, California

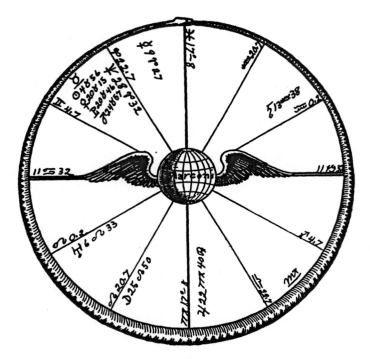

MARCHESE GUGLIELMO MARCONI, April 25, 1874, 9:00 a.m.
11:15E. 44:15N.

Pluto, planet of radio, conjunction Venus and Mars, square Saturn, square Moon in house of messages (3rd), trine Jupiter.

Uranus, planet of invention, opposition Saturn, square Sun, trine Mercury, planet of communication, in house of honor (10th).

1896, patented first wireless telegraph apparatus: Sun square Moon *r*, in house of messages (3rd); Sun P. Uranus, planet of invention; Mars sextile Mercury *r*, planet of communication, in house of honor (10th).

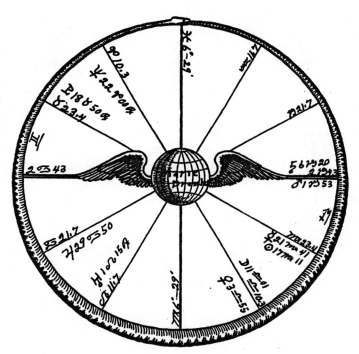

MARIE DRESSLER, November 9, 1871, 7:18 p.m. 78:10W. 44N.

Became famous as a screen actress after 55 years of age: Venus in its home sign in house of late life (4th), conjunction Moon in house of entertainment (5th), sextile Uranus in house of money (2nd).

At about 55, under Sun conjunction Saturn *r*, following Sun square Moon *r* and Mercury square Moon *r*, without funds, ready to give up, and no hope of a career. Under Venus sextile Jupiter *p*, went to an astrologer who gave her hope; told her fame and fortune ahead.

Died June 28, 1934, of cancer: Sun square Neptune *p*, Sun semi-square Saturn *r*.

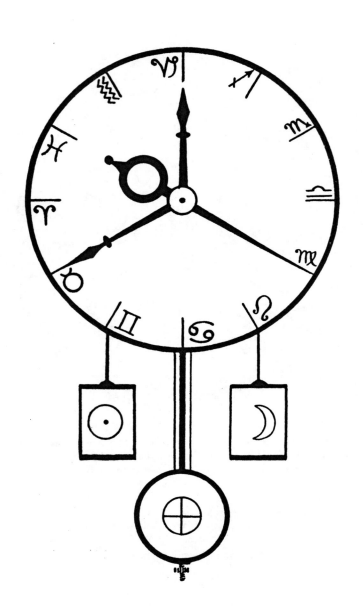

DOCTRINE OF NATIVITIES

OW that it has been shown that astral vibrations from the planets have such an important and far-reaching influence upon all life, the next step is to indicate more precisely how these vibrations affect humanity.

Yet the reader should not be given the impression that the destiny of the soul commences at its birth into human life, and that planetary influences operating at this birth are determined by chance. Therefore, it seems advisable first to outline the old Hermetic teachings in regard to the soul.

If the old Hermetic Law of Correspondences holds true—"As it is below, so it is above; as on the earth, so in the sky"—then not only the astral world, but the spiritual world, the angelic world, and the celestial world, are subject to the same seven-fold division as the physical world. In other words, the things and entities of these worlds are, even as the things and entities of earth, subject to planetary rulership. Of course, in the higher worlds the vibrations are transmitted by finer substances than the astral, but nevertheless, the entities of these realms belong to definite planetary families. All those things on any plane that are ruled by a certain planet —transmit that planet's influence more freely than any other—are said to belong to its planetary family.

Souls are no exception to this, and at the moment of differentiation in the higher realms each belongs to a certain planetary family.

I may not here speak of the angelic parenthood of souls or of the circumstances surrounding their first existence as differentiated entities. These things are explained in Course II—Astrological Signatures. I may here mention, however, that at its first existence as a soul it is endowed with a definite polarity, or quality. After its differentiation the life-impulse —that impulse which we observe causing all forms of life to struggle to live—carries the soul down through fleeting forms in the lower spiritual world, down through other fleeting and elemental forms in the astral world, and finally enables it to incarnate in the mineral realm of a planet.

Do not think that the rocks and metals are devoid of life. Professor Chunder Bose[1], through extensive experiments, has demonstrated that metals, for instance, are sensitive, may be put to sleep, may be intoxicated, or may be killed. The difference between their sensitiveness and that of higher forms of life is one of degree, due to less complex organization. The idea that I wish to convey here, however, is not merely that rocks and grass and trees as well as animals are endowed with souls, but that the soul evolves through these different forms.

The Astral Body Is Built of Stellar Cells and Stellar Structures.—In its descent to incarnate in the mineral, and in its ascent through innumerable lower forms of physical life, the soul has experiences of different kinds. The awareness and emotions accompanying these experiences build thought-elements into the high-velocity, or stellar, body. Through other experiences these thought-elements become organized as stellar cells, and these in turn into dynamic stellar structures.

Thoughts, in the sense I here use the term, embrace every form of consciousness and include the sensations felt by even the lowest forms of life. All life-forms react to environment through an awareness which builds mental elements into their finer forms. And a birth-chart—even the birth-chart of a primitive creature—is a map of the character, that is, of the thought-organizations of the finer form, as these have been constructed up to the moment of physical birth.

Living physical matter is composed of protoplasm, which is a combination of chemical elements. And the inner-plane, astral, or stellar, body of every living creature is composed of psychoplasm, formed of thought-elements in various kinds of combinations.

The physical body is built of cells of protoplasm and their secretions; and the astral body, wherein resides the soul, or character, or unconscious mind, as it is variously called, is built of thought-cells, or stellar-cells, as they also are termed. These stellar-cells are not all alike; but are composed of thought-elements of various kinds and in different proportions. They, in turn, enter into the formation of stellar structures, just as the physical cells are organized into the bony structure, the muscular structure, the nervous structure, etc., of the physical body.

Due to its original Polarity, the soul, through the Law of Affinity—the Law that Like attracts Like—builds a form of similar polarity. Its experiences in this form add thought-elements and thought-cells to its astral body. Therefore, as a result of living for a time in this form it possesses qualities that it did not have before. And these qualities, after it has passed through a period of assimilation on the astral plane, cause it to be attracted to, and enable it to mold and function in, an organism of more complex structure.

The soul, then, after it starts on its pilgrimage to matter and back to spirit again, at every step of its journey is governed by the Law of Affinity. That is, the kind of an external form it is attracted to on the physical plane depends upon the thought-organization (thought signifying any type of consciousness) of its astral form. The thought-organization of its astral form depends upon the various experiences it has previously had, each adding thought-elements and aiding to organize definite thought-cells and thought structures in the astral form. And these thought-cells and thought structures, which in reality are stored up experiences gained in other forms, give it the ability to handle the life processes, and thus build about it the new and more complex body to which it is now attracted.

The soul accomplishes its evolution, therefore, by being attracted to one form, dwelling for a time in it and undergoing certain experiences, then repelling this form and passing to the astral world. We speak of this repelling of the physical form and passing to the astral plane as death.

Then on the astral plane there is a period of existence during which other experiences are added, and the physical experiences are assimilated and still further organized. These assimilated experiences—derived from both the physical world and the astral world—persisting as stellar-cells and stellar structures in the astral body, give it the ability when cyclic law again attracts it to earth to attach itself to the forming crystal, the spore, the divided cell, or the fertilized seed that forms the physical conditions for the growth of a new physical entity. These experiences in directing the life processes that molded some simpler form in the past, also give it the unconscious, or astral, intelligence which enables it to organize about itself, or grow, the more complex life-form which it now animates.

I speak of intelligence advisedly. We are all too apt to take for granted the myriad wonders performed by the plants and insects and animals about us. To be sure, the intelligence they display is not on a level with that exercised by humanity. Yet from the same soil and air one plant will subtract, as in the case of the common red clover, the material to build a head of long-tubed flowers, painting them rose and purple as flaming advertisements to the bumble bees upon which the fertilization and consequent life of the species depends; while another plant subtracts the material, as in the case of the common white sage, for a shrub whose foliage is mostly white, instead of green, and whose flowers are white with very short tubes, easily accessible to the honey bees, and so exposed as to attract them, and thus use them as carriers of the fertilizing pollen. Plants also are far more sensitive than is usually supposed. They possess energy very similar to the nerve currents of higher animal life. The difference between the sense of feeling in plants and that in animals is one of degree. This has been adequately and scientifically demonstrated by Professor Chunder Bose[2].

Economic problems that still perplex humanity, such as the division of labor, have been solved by the ants and the bees. The orb weaver spider thoroughly tests his base line, then produces radial lines that are as accurately spaced as if drawn by a human architect. The oriole builds a hanging basket nest that any basket-maker might envy, and the wasps here in California anticipated cold storage. They sting spiders in such a manner as to paralyze them without producing death, and with them they fill the nests in which they lay their eggs, that the young may have fresh meat to eat during the larval stage. A thousand other instances of the intelligence of plants and animals might be cited. We may call it instinct if we wish, but this instinct is the expression of an intelligent adaptation of a means to an end.

Neither does this instinct spring into existence spontaneously. It is the result of experiences which are added to the thought-cells of the astral body. The organization of its astral form is responsible for the soul being attracted to the species of life which it is to animate. The physical sperm and germ, or cell-life, that are the commencement of the new physical form, also have an astral counterpart. And through the thought-cells associated with the genes —those portions of the reproductive cell handed down from generation to generation—race characteristics add their experiences, or mental elements, to the astral body of the entity that uses these cells as a physical basis of life. Thus certain race experiences are communicated to the astral body of each entity incarnating in the species.

The entity cannot incarnate in the species, however, until it has had such experiences in lower forms of life as will give it the unconscious, or astral, intelligence to build up the new physical form it is to occupy. Even the food of the higher forms of life has had enough experience in cell-building that it more readily and intelligently performs that function again. Bacteria are the lowest forms of life above the minerals, and certain bacteria can draw their sustenance directly from inorganic minerals. Plant life does this with greater difficulty, and the nitrates generated by bacteria, and the humus—decomposed organic life—in the soil are a great aid to thrifty growth. This is because the astral counterparts of such organic products have already had some experience with life processes, and therefore the more readily perform these functions.

For this reason it is impractical for chemists to make food. The chemist can make bread that contains just the correct amount of each chemical element. But if this bread is to sustain life, in some manner these elements must be given the intelligence usually acquired through the experience of growth.

They must be forced at once from the kindergarten, as it were, to high-school intelligence.

Each Cell Has a Soul.—Each cell is an entity, and possesses an intelligence of its own. It may thus be said to be the expression of the soul. It has recently been estimated that there are about as many cells in the human body as there are suns in our galaxy—possibly 40,000,000,000. However, to bring our comparison nearer home, let us say there are 140,000,000 people in the United States. Now each person in the United States has a soul, and lives his own life. The United States forms the opportunity for him to live and evolve such qualities as he can. Likewise the physical body of man affords the opportunity for its numerous population of cell-life to undergo evolution. The President of the United States governs the inhabitants of the United States in much the same manner that the soul of man governs the cell life comprising his body. And as the mind of the President is not the aggregate of the 140,000,000 minds he governs, neither is the soul of man the aggregate of the minds of the cells comprising his body. And were the comparison drawn still closer, the soul of man would be likened to an imperial ruler to whom the subject cells should give unquestioning obedience.

The reproductive cells which unite to furnish the physical conditions by which a human soul may build about itself a physical body, each may be said to have a soul. But the souls, or intelligences stored in the astral forms of these reproductive cells are, like other cell life, undergoing their own evolution, and they do not become the soul of the child. The soul of the incarnating child has its own astral form, in which are stored as organizations of stellar-cells, all the experiences of its past.

The union of the sperm and germ furnish the conditions for it to become attached to the physical cells, and through cell division to build up about it a human form. The heredity genes in these reproductive cells form the physical link by which race and family characteristics, stored up in the stellar cells of their astral counterparts, are transmitted to the astral body of the child. These race and family characteristics are experiences which are handed on from generation to generation, even as human traditions are passed from one to another by word of mouth. They are thus acquired by the incarnating soul through mental experience. They are experiences derived through the astral rather than through the physical. But as we shall later discern, experiences coming from the astral plane are quite as effective as those coming from the physical.

The soul that incarnates in human form has evolved up through innumerable lower forms of life, at each step gaining new experiences that enable it to be attracted to, and more or less successfully build about itself, a higher form. It now, along with other souls, exists on the astral plane. Whenever there is a ripened ovule in the female organism, one of the conditions is fulfilled for attracting a soul from the astral plane. The intense emotions of the sexual union raise the parents' vibrations to a state where they unconsciously are closely in touch with the astral plane. They actually attract entities from the astral plane to them at this time that correspond to the plane of their desires and emotions and the harmony or discord between them. They contact energies at this time that they do not at any other, which makes it exceedingly important that the motives be lofty and pure.

This astral plane, inhabited as it is by innumerable entities and forms of life, is not away off somewhere in space. It is all about us, and it requires but the proper conditions to be contacted at any time. Observation indicates, however, that astral substance does not communicate motion directly to physical substance. The difference in velocity between the two planes seems to be too great for such direct transmission. But electromagnetism, whose velocity seems to lie between them, performs the function of transmitting energy from the physical to the astral, and from the astral to the physical.

To be able to affect physical substance, an astral entity must utilize electromagnetic energy that already is associated with physical substance. Certain persons emanate electromagnetic energy in large volume, and in such a form that it can be used to transmit astral motions to atomic matter. Astral entities then use this electromagnetic energy for the production of supernormal physical phenomena. And the person furnishing the excess of electromagnetic energy is called a Medium.

It is this electromagnetic energy that constitutes the vital principle of all physical life. When associated with minerals it is called Mineral Magnetism. As the vital element in vegetable life, binding together the thought-cells and the physical cells and furnishing the motive power for the various vegetative functions, it is known as Vegetable Magnetism. In the animal kingdom it binds together the astral and the physical body, constitutes the vital energy, and is known as Animal Magnetism. In man it performs a like function, and is known as Personal Magnetism. Its quality depends upon the organization of the physical life it vitalizes. It persists only so long as the astral counterpart and the physical are held together, forming the means by which energy is conveyed from the one to the other. At the death of the organism this electromagnetic counterpart, or electromagnetic organization, quickly dissipates as the physical particles disintegrate.

Now, nerve currents are electric energies. And when the intense vibrations of sexual union create an electromagnetic vortex, this also creates a vortex in astral substance, and the field of force so created, if there is a ripened ovule in the female organism, attracts the soul of a child of corresponding vibration.

That is, the souls on the astral plane, that have evolved through the various lower forms of life to a point where they are now ready for human incarnation, vary as greatly in quality as do the people of the world which they become. This variance is due to their having had a different polarity at differentiation, which in the course of evolution attracted them to widely different experiences, and these divergent experiences organized different thought-cells in their astral bodies.

From the cosmic standpoint such variety seems necessary, for if all had the same experiences, all would become fitted for the same task in cosmic construction, and it seems that cosmic needs are such as to require souls whose educations bring out a wide variety of talents. But however that may be, the astral bodies of different souls have been differently organized through experiences, and the vibrations of the parents at the time of union attract a soul whose astral body corresponds in vibratory rate to the vibrations set in motion by the parents. Even should there be no physical union of the parents—for the astral plane is ever ready to utilize whatever conditions permit the physical incarnation of the life-forms which crowd it—if conception takes place, it is the vibratory rates of the parents, imparted to the sperm and germ, that determine the type of soul which is able to become attached to the fertilized cell.

If the general plane of the parents' thoughts are low, and particularly if they are on a low plane during union, the soul attracted will be of corresponding low moral bias. If their love vibrations are exalted, and the general level of their thoughts and aspirations high, a soul of high spiritual qualities will be attracted. The mental abilities of the soul attracted, as distinct from the moral, depend more upon the intensity of the union. And the physical strength and vitality depend more upon the harmony between the parents. The soul thus attracted is magnetically attached at the climax of the union to the physical ovule through the electromagnetic field then formed.

The positive electric energies which are the foundation of the future child's vitality are furnished by the father. They are strong or weak as he is or is not virile and intense at the time of union. The receptive magnetic energies which are the foundation of the future child's constitution and general health are furnished by the mother. They are strong or weak as she is, or is not, virile and intense at the time of union.

Upon the harmony between the parents, and the balance in intensity, depend the physical balance and in a measure the general success and happiness of the future child. That is, any discord or lack of balance between the parents in general, and especially at the time of union, will attract a soul in whose astral form are similar qualities. And these discordant thought-cells in its astral body will during life attract inharmony in environment and inharmonious events. Did parents but more fully understand the importance of complete harmony between them, certain souls now born into human form would be compelled to evolve higher upon the astral plane before incarnating, and there would be fewer children born with improper equipment for life.

When conception takes place the astral form of the soul becomes permanently attached to the united sperm and germ. The electromagnetic energy furnished by the father becomes the vital force, and that furnished by the mother becomes the magnetic force, and together they form the electromagnetic form. Through the medium of this electromagnetic energy

the astral form attracts the physical particles in the
process of growth in such a manner as nearly as
possible to build a physical counterpart of the astral
form. The astral form is the mold which the physical particles strive to fill in detail, even as hot metal
will take the form of the mold into which it is poured.
In so far as the physical materials at hand will permit, the physical body grows into an exact likeness of
the astral body.

The child, during the period of gestation, has
entered an environment largely influenced by the
thoughts and feelings of the mother. Both the physical and the astral bodies of mother and child are
closely associated. There is a constant exchange of
energies between them. As a consequence mothers
frequently notice that their natures and dispositions
change markedly during pregnancy. This is due to
the astral vibrations of the child communicating
themselves to the mother. If there is a marked discord between the astral makeup of the mother and
the child, she will suffer from this discord. In this
case the discord may not belong either to the mother
or to the child except that their association, due to
difference in vibratory rates in their astral bodies,
sets up discords.

But of far more importance than the temporary
influence of the child upon the disposition of the
mother is the mother's influence upon the unborn
child. The child's astral form at this stage is unusually plastic and receptive to vibrations. Thus it is
that cases are known in which the mother kept the
image of a loved one in her mind during gestation,

and the child when born resembled in features this loved one rather than the father or the mother. A sudden strong desire during pregnancy, or a sudden fright, sometimes results in a birthmark more or less resembling the object causing it. Such fright, when extreme, has been known to deform the offspring. In this intimate relation between mother and child during pregnancy the mother has a wonderful power for good. Her thoughts, her emotions, and her desires are the environment in which the child is living. They communicate rates of motion to its astral form, modifying the thought organizations already there. Upon the thought organization of the astral form, thus modified by the mother's influence, depends the character of the child when born and the events of its life.

It is not necessary here to enter into a discussion of the Prenatal Epoch, as the theory of the relation between the time of conception and the time of birth is called, for this is treated in lesson No. 117. Nevertheless, it should be pointed out that gestation is under astrological law, and that the child will not be born and live until the astral vibrations at that place set up by planetary positions correspond in pitch, tone, harmony and discord with the astral vibrations of the child then born. It is not to be supposed that this vibratory correspondence is so strict as to allow no latitude. For instance, in tone, the vibrations between certain limits all are said to produce middle C. The color red, likewise, is not a set number of vibrations per second, but those vibrations within a certain range. In the case of birth, however, if the difference between the vibrations of the astral body and those of the planetary influences at the time of birth are extensive, the child suffers, and if too great it will die under the first discordant Progressed Aspect. Hence it is that instrumental deliveries and artificial births may cause an entity to function through a form incapable of responding to its internal nature. Yet there are other times than at the end of the nine-month period, notably at seven months from conception, when the vibrations set up by the planets correspond closely enough with the astral form of the child for it to be born and live to a ripe old age.

The Birth-Chart Accurately Maps the Character as It Has Been Built Up to the Moment of Birth.— While there is a certain range of vibratory rates within which the similarity between those of the character and those in the sky is close enough that the child then born will live, nevertheless this similarity—as careful analysis of tens of thousands of birth-charts by our Research Department proves— is always close enough that the outstanding factors of character are accurately mapped in the birth-chart.

And as not only the abilities, but every event of life, is an expression of, or is attracted by, those thought organizations which comprise the character, the birth-chart gives a clear picture of the life if nothing special is done to change the character. That is, as all that happens is the result of character, the only manner in which the destiny can be changed is to change the character. Furthermore, as destiny is the outcome of character, and through intelligently directed effort the character can be changed, the life indicated by the chart of birth—which is merely a map of the character with which the individual is born—can be markedly altered in any direction desired.

As indicated in lesson No. 41, scientific astrology need concern itself with but four sets of factors: 1. The 12 zodiacal signs and their 36 decanate subdivisions. 2. The 10 planets. 3. The 12 mundane houses. 4. The 10 aspects. In that lesson it was indicated what each of these four sets of factors represents as an influence from without. Now, therefore, let us consider, that we may the better understand how the character and thus the fortune can be altered in any direction desired, what each of these factors maps in the astral body.

Signs Map the Zones of the Astral Body.—Aries always maps the region of the head, Taurus the region of the neck and ears, Gemini the hands and arms, etc. They also map the series to which the thought-cells in the compartments of the astral body coincident with these zones belong. Thus the thought-cells in the Aries zone belong to the I Am series, those in the Taurus zone to the I Have series, those in the Gemini zone to the I Think series, etc.

Mundane Houses Map the Compartments of the Astral Body.—The astral, or inner-plane body, is divided not merely into zones as is the physical body —head, neck, arms and hands, heart and back, etc. —but is also separated into 12 different compartments. And these compartments of the astral body are not located in reference to the zones of the astral body the same in different persons. That is, compartment 1 may largely lie in the Aries zone, the Gemini zone, or some of the other zones, according to the character of the individual. This relationship is indicated by the manner in which the signs are arranged in relation to the houses in the particular birth-chart.

Yet whatever zone covers it, experiences relating to health and the personality build their thought-elements into the 1st compartment; experiences relating to personal property build their thought-elements into the 2nd compartment; experiences relating to short journeys and brethren build their elements into the 3rd compartment; experiences relating to the home build their thought-elements into the 4th compartment; experiences relating to love affairs, entertainment and children build their thought-elements into the 5th compartment—and so on in such a manner that every department of life builds by its experiences, thought-cells in one of the 12 compartments of the astral body.

In a birth-chart the houses accurately map these 12 compartments of the astral body. Each house of the birth-chart, therefore, maps the thought-cells relating to one department of the life. As what comes into the life, and whether it comes fortunately or as a misfortune, is determined wholly by the amount of activity and the harmony or discord of the thought-cells in the astral body relating to that department of life, the houses of a birth-chart accurately map what may be expected if nothing special is done about it, from each department of the life.

That is, what happens is due to the activity of the thought-cells working from the high-velocity plane; and if we know how they are organized and energized we can discern the events they will attract to the individual in whose finer form they make their abode.

Planets Map Dynamic Stellar Structures Which are Also Receiving Sets. — The thought-cells of a particular type which have had added to them experiences of greatest intensity, and through repetition of similar experiences the greatest volume of energy, become organized through these intense and closely related experiences into a stellar structure of a highly active nature. We call such an energetic group of thought-cells in the astral body a Dynamic Stellar Structure. And in the birth-chart it is always mapped by the planet ruling the thought-element which is most active in it.

To put it another way, those experiences which are most intense and belong to a given planetary family build a highly dynamic organization of thought-cells in some particular region of the astral body; and this energetic organization of stellar-cells is always mapped in the birth-chart by the planet most closely related to the experiences which are responsible for its construction. Such a dynamic stellar structure acts as a receiving set for transmitting to the thought-cells of the astral body the vibrations of the planet mapping it in the birth-chart.

Aspects Map Stellar Aerials Which Pick Up, Radio Fashion, Invisible Energies. — Experiences, however, are not isolated events, but though the Law of Association (see Course V) are related to other experiences. Events that affect one department of life also frequently affect other departments. Furthermore, experiences are pleasant or painful, that is, harmonious or discordant; and it is the amount of harmony built into the thought-cells thus formed that determines the fortune they will attract to the individual; and it is the amount of discord built into the thought-cells so formed that determines the misfortune they will attract to the individual. In other words, if they feel happy, they work from their high-velocity plane to attract good fortune; but if they feel mean, they work with equal diligence to attract misfortune.

These relations between types of experiences of sufficient energy to form dynamic stellar structures, build lines across the astral body from one dynamic structure to other dynamic structures with which experience has thus associated them. Such a line forms a ready avenue by which the compartment of the astral body at one end is able to transmit energy to the compartment of the astral body at the other end. That is, departments of life so associated continue throughout life, if nothing special is done about it, to have an influence of a particular kind over each other.

Such a line, by its length, also indicates whether the two compartments are associated harmoniously or inharmoniously, and thus whether the thought-elements mapped by the planet at either end have entered into a harmonious or discordant thought-cell compound.

But in addition to this, each such line acts as a stellar aerial to pick up, radio fashion, the energies of similar quality radiated from the planets. That is, if it is of a length suitable only to picking up discord, it will pick the energies of the planets mapped at each end only so loaded with static that this energy disturbs the thought-cells in a very disagreeable manner. But if it is of such a length as to pick up the energies mapped at each end harmoniously, it delivers these planetary energies to the thought-cells at either end in such pleasing quality as to cause them to work from their high-velocity plane to attract fortunate conditions into the life.

These lines across the astral body, which, unless something special is done to change them, all through life pick up, radio fashion, planetary-energy, thought-energy, and character-energy radiated from objects, in a particular manner, are called PERMANENT STELLAR AERIALS. They are mapped in the birth-chart by the ASPECTS.

Character Constantly Reacts to the Forces of Its Environment. — Environment constantly stimulates changes in all life-forms; and chief among these environmental forces are the invisible radiations from the planets. As the planets move forward after birth through the signs of the zodiac the energies fall upon the zone of the astral body governed by the sign they are passing through. And it seems that the astral body of a child is more plastic and receptive to these astral vibrations during the early days and months of its life than when older. Furthermore, the energies then received do not spend their force at once, but are liberated through cycles.

In the same way that we determine the cycles governing the different stages of development of the embryo in a duck-egg, and can thus make definite predictions from this knowledge, or as we can predict that a certain strain of corn when planted will be out of the ground in so many days, in so many weeks will tassel, in so many months will be in the milk, and that one hundred days from the time placed in the ground will be mature; we can also determine the cycles governing similar releases of energy stored in the human astral body. That method is through observation.

The Three Releases of Energy. — Observation acquaints us with the fact that there are three distinct releases of energy, each measured by its own cycle. The most important such release is at the ratio of the movements of the planets during one day after birth releasing energy then stored during one year of life. The next most important such release of energy is at the ratio of the movements of the planets during one month after birth releasing energy then stored during one year of life. And the least important such release of energy is at the ratio of the movements of the planets during one day after birth releasing energy then stored during the same day of life.

Because the mapping of these three methods of

energy storage and release is done by moving, or "progressing" the planets through the degrees and signs of the birth-chart, the releases of energy after this manner are called Progressions. They are comparable to the releases of energy of a clock which has an hour hand, a minute hand, and a second hand.

Energy is stored up in the clock by being imparted to a spring, or by weights being lifted. The energy stored up in the clock weights is not released all at once—no more so than the energy stored up by planetary movements immediately following birth. In the case of the clock it is released by the cyclic movement of the pendulum or other device; and in the case of the birth-chart it is released by the cyclic motion of our earth about the Sun.

The Hour hand of the clock corresponds to the important day for a year ratio of release in the astral body, which is the ratio of Major Progressions.

The Minute hand of the clock corresponds to the next most important month for a year ratio of release in the astral body, which is the ratio of Minor Progressions.

The Second hand of the clock corresponds to the least important day for a day ratio of release in the astral body, which is the ratio of Transits.

As the planets thus move forward after birth, regardless of aspect, or aerial, they store up energy which when released according to the ratios of progression, imparts their type of energy to the zone where they are shown by progression; and this gives

the thought-cells of the indicated region more than
their normal activity. And this is true whether the
planet moves through the sign by Major Progression, by Minor Progression or by Transit; although
the amount of energy thus imparted and released by
Major Progression is far greater.

**Progressed Aspects Map Temporary Stellar
Aerials.** — From what has now been said I think it
will be clear that the function of Progressions is to
map those structural changes which take place in the
astral body, in obedience to cyclic law, that permit
energies from the planets at definite and predictable
times, to reach certain groups of thought-cells in
volume enough to give them extraordinary activities.

When a planet progressing according to one of
the three indicated ratios forms an aspect with a
planet in the birth-chart, or with another major progressed planet, the energy-release then builds across
the astral body a line which acts as an aerial which
picks up and transmits to its two terminals, energy
of the type of the two planets involved in the aspect.
Experience proves that these temporary stellar
aerials, mapped by progressed aspects, while their
influence may be felt over a somewhat longer period,
are seldom clear cut enough to pick up sufficient
energy to bring an event into the life either before
or after the planets are within one degree of the
perfect aspect.

These temporary stellar aerials thus formed by
the cyclic release of energy, have a length indicated
by the aspect which maps them, and this determines

whether the astral energy, from any source derived
—thought-energy, and character-vibration energy as
well as planetary energy—which they pick up, will
be given a harmonious turn, or will be loaded with
discordant static.

To the extent they transmit energy which is harmonious to the stellar-cells at their terminals, are
the thought-cells there given an impetus to work to
attract favorable events. Likewise, to the extent
these temporary stellar aerials transmit energy which
is discordant to the stellar cells at their terminals,
are the thought-groups there located given an impetus to attract misfortune.

**Events Are Attracted Into the Life Only by Un-
usual Thought-Cell Activities.**—The stellar-cells of
which the astral body is composed, the more active
of which are organized into dynamic stellar structures which are mapped by the planets in the birth-
chart, have a certain intelligence of their own, and
work from the high-velocity plane to attract into the
life conditions and events corresponding to the way
they feel.

When they receive no additional energy from any
source they have only the amount and kind of activity
indicated by the birth-chart. It is only when, from
some source—astrological vibrations, thought vibrations, or the character vibrations of objects—they
receive an additional energy supply that their activity
is greater than the normal thus shown.

The whole problem of predicting the nature and
time of events by natal astrology, therefore, is to

ascertain the time when certain groups of stellar-cells within the astral body will receive additional energy; and in what volume and in what harmony or discord it will reach them. And it is this that a knowledge of Progressed Aspects enables us to do.

Because, except some special effort based on astrological knowledge is made, the stellar cells of the astral body receive additional energy of sufficient intensity only when Progressed Aspects indicate Temporary Stellar Aerials have been formed across the astral body; events apart from the normal everyday trend of the life are attracted only when Progressed Aspects are present within one degree of perfect. And as the temporary stellar aerial thus mapped is plainly associated with certain compartments of the astral body, as mapped by the houses of the birth-chart influenced by the aspect, the department of life to which the thought-cells belong which are thus given additional activity is readily apparent.

The families to which the thought-cells belong, and therefore their type of activity — aggressive, social, timid and cunning, etc.—are indicated by the planets involved in the Progressed Aspect. The department of life to which they will give increased activity is shown by the house rulership of the planets involved in the Progressed Aspect. And — taking also into consideration the normal harmony or discord of the thought-cells thus given activity — the nature of a Progressed Aspect determines whether, and to what extent, the unusual activity of the thought-cells thus given energy will be favorable or unfavorable in the type of events they attract.

Events Shown by Progressed Aspects Are Not Inevitable but Are Subject to Intelligent Control.— While it is true that the structure of the astral body responds to cyclic law and tends to build lines, or temporary stellar aerials across the astral body, at the time energy is released through Progressed Aspects; it is also true that the astral body, unconscious mind, or character, as it is variously called, is equally responsive to properly directed thoughts and emotions.

Anything that can be done in the way of structural changes and adding energy to thought-cells by planets, can be done equally well through persistently directed thoughts and cultivated experiences. The thought-cells were built into the astral body in the first place through states of consciousness stimulated by environment. They were not built there by the environment, but by the mental reaction to it. And by cultivating a proper reaction to planetary vibrations at the time of the release of energy by Progressed Aspects the events usually to be expected can be markedly changed in the direction desired.

A Complete Reading of a Birth-Chart.—In a complete birth-chart reading, therefore, the following seven factors should be included: 1. The person receiving the birth-chart should be told just what it represents. 2. He should be told, in connection with each department of life, what will be attracted, and why, if nothing special is done about it. 3. He should be informed as to the best methods to follow to change the destiny of each department of life in the desired direction. 4. He should be told what a progressed aspect represents. 5. He should be told what events each progressed aspect during the period covered may be expected to attract if nothing special is done about it. 6. In connection with each progressed aspect during the period covered he should be told the very best method of causing the energies then present to attract, not what they otherwise would, but what he desires. 7. To show that the basis for such information is at hand he should be given an accurately erected chart of the time of day of birth.

---

[1] Response in the Living and Non-Living.
[2] Plant Response.

DOCTRINE OF MEDIUMSHIP

Serial No. 43

THE CHURCH OF LIGHT
Box 1525, Los Angeles 53, California

Printed in U.S.A.

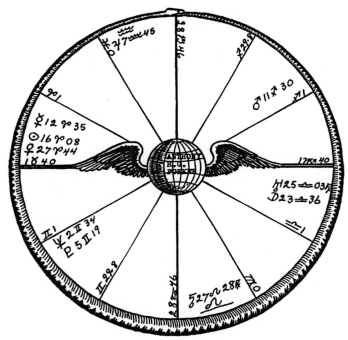

ANTHONY H. G. FOKKER, April 6, 1890, 7:00 a.m., 106:45E. 6:30S. Data given in biography.

1906, made up mind to build plane: Sun semi-sextile Neptune *r*.

1910, built plane: Mercury conjunction Venus *p*.

1912, unsuccessful in selling plane: Sun square Jupiter *r*.

1914, Fokker planes win war victories: Mars trine Mercury *r*.

1916, designed triplane: Mercury conjunction Neptune *r*.

1922, joined forces with General Motors: Venus trine Jupiter *r*, Mars sextile Jupiter *p*.

1930, Tri-motors Fokker circumnavigates globe: Mercury sextile Mercury *r*.

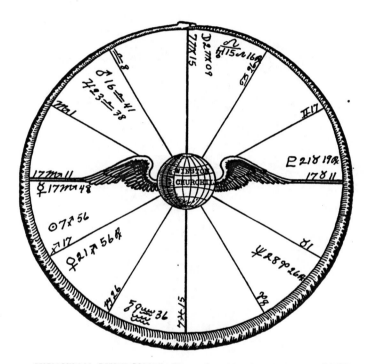

WINSTON CHURCHILL, November 30, 1874, 6:00 a.m., LMT.,
6:18W. 53:21N. Data furnished by a relative.

1895, with armed forces in Cuba; Sun trine Neptune *r*, Mars
square Neptune *r*.

1898, medal for action with Nile Expeditionary Forces: Sun
trine Moon *r*, Sun sextile Mars *p*.

1899, taken prisoner in South Africa and escaped: Sun semi-
square Mercury.

1915, disastrous Gallipoli campaign: Mercury square Mars *r*.

1930, First Lord of Admiralty: Mars opposition Pluto *r*.

1940, War Prime Minister of England: Mercury sextile Neptune
r, Venus trine Neptune *r*, Mercury sextile Venus *p*.

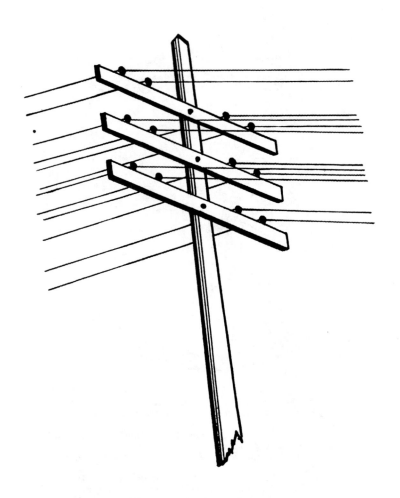

DOCTRINE OF MEDIUMSHIP

IT IS NOT within the province of these lessons on mediumship to offer proof that the numerous kinds of psychic phenomena considered are genuine, but to cite where such proof may be found and to explain them according to the findings of Hermetic Initiates.

The most convincing proof, to be sure, is that based upon personal experience, and thousands are having such proof each day. But my personal experience, or your personal experience, has very little weight with those who have had no like occurrence. We must refer such to the innumerable cases of psychic phenomena, belonging to all classes, which have been painstakingly collected by men of international scientific standing and integrity. A host of such phenomena have been witnessed and critically analyzed under such circumstances as to make fraud or illusion impossible. The person nowadays who denies a wide variety of psychic phenomena, ranging from telepathy, clairvoyance and premonition to, and including, haunted houses and materializations, is merely behind the times and ignorant. Of the many men of international scientific reputation who have seriously investigated such psychic phenomena I know of not a single one who remains unconvinced of their genuineness.

Since these lessons were first written there has been a vast amount of additional proof published. In 1923 Charles Richet, Professor of Physiology in the University of Paris, came out with a book of over six hundred pages, "Thirty Years of Psychical Research," in which he gives a large number of carefully verified instances of the numerous types of psychic phenomena. In 1920 there appeared in English, "Phenomena and Materialization," by Baron Von Schrenk Notzing, a large volume illustrated with two hundred twenty-five photographs of spirit materializations. The conditions under which these photographs were obtained were of the strictest nature, and not only afford positive proof that materializations actually take place, but yield much new knowledge of the manner in which they are formed.

In 1922 there was published, "Death and Its Mystery," by Camille Flammarion, a large collection of authentic instances of telepathy, clairvoyance, the sight of future events, etc. Also in 1922, another book of the same series, "At the Moment of Death," by Flammarion, was published. This book contains a large collection of well verified cases of phantasms of the living, apparitions of the dying, psychic warnings of approaching death, deaths announced by blows from invisible agents, and other psychic manifestations of the dying. In 1923 the third of this series, "After Death," by Flammarion, appeared. It contains a large collection of verified cases where the dead have returned according to previous agreement, and of other manifestations and apparitions after death. The latter are arranged according to the length of time after death that they appeared, and constitute conclusive proof that the dead do sometimes return, the length of time elapsing after death before the return being any time from a few minutes to thirty years.

Finally, in 1924, "Haunted Houses," by Flammarion, was published. This book is a collection of a very large number of cases of genuine hauntings, and forever disposes of the question of whether or not there actually are haunted houses. Camille Flammarion, who has attained an international reputation as a scientist through his astronomical work, has been gathering data on psychic subjects for the last fifty years. In 1899 he intensified his efforts in this direction, and put forth a wide and systematic effort to collect well authenticated cases of psychic phenomena. Up to that time he had received some 500 psychic observations. Since then he has received more than 5,600 different psychic observations. The Psychic Research Societies of France, England, Italy, Germany and other countries have published about as many more that have come to his notice, so that he had some ten or eleven thousand different psychic observations from which to draw conclusions.

Facts are always of greater weight than theories. Here we have facts; innumerable facts; verified facts; incontrovertible facts; all testifying that psychic phenomena take place, and a great many of them testifying that the dead survive.

It seems strange that the very religions that teach life after death are so bitter against proof being offered that such is the case. If an enlightened people are to believe in a life after death there must be some proof of it. What better proof can there be than that the dead return and manifest a personality that is recognizable? If the dead still live, why should we think there are insurmountable barriers to communicating with them? As I write no airship has flown across the Pacific Ocean. Some think such a feat impossible. But it will be done. A retrospect shows a thousand obstacles to man's achievement that were once thought insurmountable. But one by one they have been overcome. Today's psychic phenomena, it is true, is more or less sporadic and imperfect. But in spite of this, a vast proportion of it is genuine. As such it points the way to a more perfect form that may be brought under the control of the human will.

I should not omit mention of "The Case for Spirit Photography" (1923), and "The Coming of the Fairies" (1922), by A. Conan Doyle. The former book relates instances of spirit photography and is illustrated from spirit photographs. The latter is an account of an investigation of some fairies which were photographed by two little girls under such circumstances as to make fraud impossible.

There are other books and many magazine articles that have appeared in the last few years, all offering definite examples of psychic phenomena. But those mentioned will be quite conclusive to any person who can be convinced through reading about the experiences of others. To those who must have personal experience to convince them, there is always open the more arduous, but very satisfactory road of experimental investigation. Of this I feel confident; any person who will approach the problem with an unbiased mind and investigate painstakingly over a long period cannot but be satisfied both as to the reality of the various kinds of psychic phenomena and that the human personality survives death.

This being the case, the question naturally arises: how it is possible for those existing on other planes of life to manifest themselves through such phenomena, or in any manner communicate with those yet in the flesh. To answer this question we must first understand, in its broadest sense, what the term *mediumship* implies.

Take the smith who shapes a horseshoe. When the iron is placed in the fire it is cold, meaning that it has a slow molecular motion. The fire, on the other hand, has a swift molecular motion—is hot. Through contact some of the molecular motion of the fire is imparted to the iron, increasing its molecular motion. It, in turn, becomes hot, which is but another way of stating that it is a passive agent of the fire in the forge and has become a medium for the transmission of its energy.

Next the smith removes the red-hot iron from the fire, places it upon the anvil, and by means of blows from a hammer shapes it to the form he desires.

He has in his mind an image of the shape it is to assume. His motor nerves respond to his mind as mediums for transmitting his thoughts to his muscles. The hammer in his hand is the medium through

which he transmits the energy of his muscles in a
particular manner to the iron he is shaping. The
iron he shapes, the fire in the forge, the hammer in
his hand, his muscles and nerves; all are mediums
through which the smith transmits a subjective form
of energy called an idea into an objective form of
energy called a horseshoe. There is an unbroken
chain of mediumship between the active thought held
in the smith's mind and the passive piece of iron that
has become a horseshoe. In each instance that which
was more active controlled and used as a medium
that which was less active. And this is one of the
fundamental laws of mediumship, that the passive is
always controlled by the active.

This law in mediumship is as fundamental as that
of the conservation of energy. Conservation of
energy not only applies to psychic matters, but is the
very Gibraltar upon which physical science rests. It
is the law that energy can never be created or destroyed. Therefore all energy existing today is derived from some preexisting form of energy.

Energy may be transformed in a thousand different ways, some of which were noticed in the case of
the smith shaping the iron, but it can never be lost
to one thing except through giving it to something
else. Thus the energy residing in the mineral and in
the carbon of the air is assimilated by plant life, and
this still later is organized into the cell life of an
animal, finally to return to the soil to be assimilated
by some other life form. The energy reaching the
earth from the sun may be stored up in plant life
and buried, subjected to great pressure which trans-

forms it into coal, and finally be dug up by man and used as fuel to generate power for use in all the intricate ways of modern manufacturing industry. In fact, a little reflection will show that the whole Solar System is but the medium through which the Sun exercises its controlling power. To be sure, as still further reflection will indicate, everything in existence from the highest spiritual beings to the dense rocks of earth are mediums for transmitting particular kinds of energy.

To sum up the extent of mediumship, without taking space to enumerate examples in proof of it, the statement may be made that the whole Universe is mediumistic in the sense of receiving and again transmitting energy, God being the One Great Controlling Power.

Now if we look about us we perceive that everything is in motion. At least a close analysis will reveal that those things which are stationary are only so because of our dull perceptions. This motion implies that something is acting as a medium for the transmission of energy. Thus positive and negative electric charges oscillating about each other may set up the particular transverse wave motions that we call light. Space then becomes the medium for the transmission of energy. It is passive to and controlled by the electric charges. Likewise, molecular motion, as heat, may be transmitted from one object to another. In this case the heat is the controlling agent, and the object receiving the heat the passive medium. Or radiant heat, which is electromagnetic motion, may be transmitted across space without a material agent, communicating motion to the molecules of physical substance, and the physical substance become hot, as when we place an object in the sunshine. The physical object then becomes the medium for the expression on the physical plane of an energy received through a non-material medium, from a distant controlling center, the sun. The radio is another instance of the power of a distant controlling influence to transmit energy though space and set up physical motions through a passive receiving medium.

The mind of man, as taught by Hermetic Science, is an organization of energy in astral and still finer substances. These astral energies may be communicated to physical substance, as was seen in the case of the smith shaping the horseshoe. Mental energies, residing as they do in substances finer than the physical, are more active than physical energies, and hence, following our fundamental law that the passive is always controlled by the active, they exercise a controlling power over the physical.

It is not the volume of energy present that determines its power to control so much as its relative activity. This relative activity may obtain by virtue of various circumstances, as when the throttle of an engine is opened, or a small shove is given to an object nicely balanced on the edge of a precipice. In such cases neither the throttle nor the shove generates the large amount of energy used. They but release in a definite direction energy that is already present. Nevertheless, at the moment they exercise controlling power the throttle and the shove relatively are more active than the energies released by them.

The human mind, also, by advantage of its intense activity, constantly releases energies already existing on the physical plane.

One is justified in saying, I believe, that man is man and not something else because he has learned how to utilize and control very numerous and complex forces and functions. The soul, which embraces all the various states of consciousness stored in his astral and spiritual makeup, is able to function through the body of man on the physical plane only because through a long period of education and effort it has learned how to control such a body.

The process of evolution is a schooling in the capture, storage, and release of energy. The physical bodies of all kinds of mundane life are the mediums through which energy previously existing is diverted into special channels by the intelligences occupying such bodies. This energy may merely be the food partaken of, which is utilized in the movements and life processes of the organism. Or it may consist of the finer astral energies radiated by the Sun and planets. But in any case the height of an organism in the evolutionary scale is determined by its power to control and intelligently direct complex energies.

The mollusks, the fishes in the sea, the amphibians, the reptiles, the birds of the air and the beasts of the field each capture, store, and release energy. They are all mediums in the sense of receiving and transmitting force. Each, however, in the order named, has improved upon the methods of the previous one in the power to control and intelligently direct this energy. Furthermore, man is superior to all other forms upon the earth, not by virtue of the volume of energy within his body, but by his ability to control and intelligently direct himself. So long as he has the power intelligently to direct himself, he is able to utilize not only the energy of his own body, but a multitude of other energies by which he is surrounded.

The whole struggle for survival is but a struggle of the species and the individual to preserve and perpetuate the control of its organism. Any tendency, therefore, to relinquish the control of the human body or to permit another to control it, tends toward the destruction of the individuality.

This is immediately apparent from a study of material biology only. But when we consider the methods by which a soul evolves through form after form, in each learning how to control some new function and process, until at last it has had experience enough in intelligently controlling energy to be able to incarnate in human shape, we see from a new angle that the control of one's organism is perhaps the most vital thing in human life.

That which people who are striving to accomplish anything continually do is to endeavor to acquire greater and greater control over their own bodies, their own energies, and their own thoughts. To be unusually accomplished in any direction means that an unusual amount of control has been gained over some set of muscles, or over some mental process, or both. Control over self is the first requisite to success, and the greater the control the more certain the success. If there is good control in one direction and lack of it in another, there will be good prospects of success in the direction of the control, and none in the direction of lack of control.

If we but reflect upon the steps that must be taken by the child in learning to control and intelligently direct himself before he is capable of making his own way in the world we will perceive how vastly important is this element of control. It is only through repeated effort over considerable time that he learns to talk. At first he cannot control and properly direct the muscles of the tongue and mouth to produce the sounds he wishes to make. Learning to walk is another process that takes considerable time. Bye and bye, through repeated effort, control is gained over the muscles used in walking. We thus might proceed with one thing after another that the child must learn, each requiring repeated effort over and over again until that nice coordination between mind and muscles is attained which enables him to perform the desired act. This laborious process of gaining control of his body on the part of the child is but a similar, though briefer, process to that followed by the whole of life in its evolutionary struggle.

We also are familiar with the fact that an acquired power is soon lost if not used. A marksman, a musician, a mathematician, all must keep in practice if they are to excel. The college athlete ten years after leaving usually is unable to do any one of many things he could easily do while in college. Even a doctor or a lawyer must keep in practice to be able to do good work. A faculty not used atrophies.

Fish that live for generations in the water of underground caverns often lose their sight. The vermiform appendix, which causes men so much trouble, appears to be but the degenerate vestige of a larger tract present in man's ancestors, which was used to break up cellulose when they ate, as do horses and cows now, grasses and vegetables having this abundant in their structure. A change of diet has caused it to be no longer used for its original purpose. Through lack of use it has grown smaller and smaller, until now it is present only in miniature.

It will be seen, I believe, without further illustrations, which could be supplied indefinitely, that the acquirement of control over one's body, or any portion of it, is at the expense of much energy, and that such control when once gained is easily lost. Further, it should be evident that as gain in control is progress, loss of control is retrogression.

Also, as control is gained by effort and practice, loss of control certainly follows lack of effort and practice. And of all forms of lack of effort toward, and practice in, self-control, the most rapid method of losing such control is to relinquish the controlling power to some other entity.

Every form of life, from its birth to its death, must struggle against the invasion of its organism and more or less complete control of it by other entities. Plants must resist various insects and parasitic forms. Note how certain insects cause the oak to grow oak-galls, distortions that are of no benefit to the tree, but benefit the insects only. Animals must resist parasites and a thousand kinds of germs, and man also must keep his body clean and vigorous if he would resist the ravages of disease.

Man, too, has had to struggle continually against autocratic powers that would enslave him physically and financially, and against religious hierarchies that would enslave his mind. Whenever any form of life ceases to resist invasion, there are always entities eager to use this loss of control for their own advantage. Whenever man has relaxed his vigilance politically, he has been despoiled. Look at history and weigh this well. Whenever man ceases to resist it, religious intolerance takes control. Read history again. Likewise, whenever man relinquishes the control of his body and mind to another he is inviting slavery to a master of whose identity he cannot be sure.

But of even greater importance is this, that every time a person delivers the control of any faculty or function to another he is undoing what it took him so long to learn to do. The control which is so vital a factor in his life was gained by getting his nerves and muscles into the habit of obeying him. Such a habit is readily destroyed. Even the habit of thinking correctly is easily superseded by the habit of permitting some other entity to do the thinking. It is so much easier. A man who has been sober all his life can become a habitual drunkard in a few weeks, and unable to remain sober. A man, likewise, who has a remarkable power of self-control built up over a lifetime can so destroy that self-control in a few weeks by permitting some other entity to use his brain and body that he finds it impossible to do what he wishes to do, and impossible to refrain from doing as the dominating entity suggests.

There is another biological law that any life-form that becomes a parasite ceases to evolve and degenerates to a lower level. No longer being under the necessity of procuring food in open competition with other forms of life, having found a way in which to live with little effort, it sinks to a lower biological level. In a manner not dissimilar, those who permit themselves to be dominated by some other intelligence, not only lose the power to control themselves, but become so dependent upon other intelligences that they fail to progress and tend physically, mentally, and morally to slip back.

The soul gained whatever control it has over the brain and physical body through organizing lines of force in the astral form. These special astral lines of force, organized by ceaseless effort to control the thoughts and actions, transmit the orders of the soul to the brain and nervous system. The electromagnetic motions thus set up cause the person to think objectively in a certain way and to act in a certain way, just as the soul dictates.

Now, however, if the soul turns the control of its brain and actions temporarily over to some other entity, this other entity, in order to exercise control, must organize lines of force in the person's astral form suitable to transmitting its orders to the person's brain and nervous system. Just as every time the person exercises control over his own actions, the lines of force in his astral body establishing such control are strengthened, so any time any foreign entity exercises control over the person such lines of force are strengthened and will the more readily enable a foreign entity to obtain and exercise controlling power.

Further, in order that the invading entity, whether it be a hypnotist on the material plane or a discarnate entity on the astral plane, may be insured against its control being interrupted inopportunely, it becomes necessary for it temporarily to resist any effort of the person to break such control. The very act of resisting the person's attempts to regain complete control of his own body directs energies toward breaking down the lines of force in the astral body by which the soul has been accustomed to control his own brain and body.

The spirit medium, therefore, who undergoes so-called development by becoming passive and permitting some discarnate entity to take control, is undoing the most important work of his life and of evolution. Instead of resisting invasion he is permitting another entity to build lines of force in his astral body that when strong enough will permit that entity to take possession of the brain and body in spite of its rightful owner any time it desires to do so. He is permitting lines of force to be established that provide an open door by which any other entity on the physical or astral plane may gain a like control over him in spite of himself. He is permitting lines of force in his astral body which he has spent so much time and effort in building, and by which he exercises control over his body and its functions, to be wantonly destroyed.

Every time a person goes wholly or partially under the control of a spirit, a mesmerist, or a hypnotist, he is assisting in the destruction of his own individuality. Permitting such control is irresponsible and disintegrative mediumship. Such practices persisted in bring the unfortunate subject or medium to a state where he is helpless to repel the invasion of his organism by any active entity, incarnate or discarnate. Irresponsible mediumship tends to destroy the will and soul.

There are various ways by which these negative states may be induced and irresponsible mediumship attained. The first requisite is to attain a blank, passive state of mind in which the soul has no point of contact with or control over the objective thoughts and actions. In developing circles the sitters are so arranged as to generate a strong current from their electromagnetic emanations, which is used by astral entities present to produce a mesmeric effect, and so hasten absolute passivity. In hypnotism the attention is fixed steadily in some direction to produce a state of abstraction in which the subject accepts without resistance any suggestion offered him.

In all these cases the divine soul ceases to act with

much force upon the unconscious mind, other lines of force being set up in it by the dominating idea or entity. It matters not whether the operator is a hypnotist, a discarnate entity, or the combined thought forms of other people with whom the subject associates, the effect is the same. He sees, hears, and desires what the operator demands. These things may be true or false, but the subject has no method of discriminating. If the controlling entity is intelligent it may impart useful information. If not, it may utter mere nonsense. In any case the subject is not exercising his own functions, but merely shadowing what some other entity wishes him to do or feel. For this he is paying a fearful price, for he is gradually losing the power to direct his own organism, and is becoming the abject slave to disintegrative forces. He is undoing what he has struggled so hard to accomplish, losing the ability to mould a form to meet his needs.

For those unfortunate individuals who have become irresponsible mediums I have only sympathy and no word of condemnation. Many of them have added to the happiness of the world by bringing comfort to those whose loved ones have passed on, and the assurance that there is a life after physical death. Many of them have submitted themselves to the most rigid tests of scientific men, and have thus provided irrefutable proof of the various kinds of psychic phenomena, proof also that is beyond denial that those who have passed through the tomb yet live. The world owes a great obligation to a host of self-sacrificing spirit mediums.

The world also owes its thanks to valiant doctors who have injected serums into their own veins to prove their effect. It owes its thanks to thousands of others who have suffered martrydom for the sake of science. Nor have I one word of objection to any person, after he has weighed the consequences well, developing the irresponsible phase of mediumship. If he is convinced he can be of greater benefit to society by permitting his individuality to be destroyed that entities from another plane may use him as an instrument by which to manifest on the physical plane, he should have full option in the matter. It is desirable, however, that all the facts be known beforehand so that those who do not wish to make such a heroic sacrifice may not be led into it under misapprehension.

If the astral plane, where disembodied entities dwell, were the abode of human beings only, the matter of surrendering self-control would not assume so serious an aspect. The thought even of surrendering the body and brain to discarnate human beings is not altogether pleasant when it is remembered that all the vicious, criminal, insane, and morbid people who die do not, for considerable time, change in their desires, tendencies, and traits. In fact, the lower strata of mankind remain very close to the earth for some time, being earth bound by their physical desires. They welcome the opportunity to realize those desires through the physical body of any mediumistic person they can seize. Many an act of crime, many a repulsive habit formed, many an erratic action, may be laid at the door of a discarnate entity who has found opportunity temporarily to get control of some person whose power of resistance is weak.

But depraved human beings, and those not depraved, are not the only astral entities by any means. Every insect, reptile, fish and mammal that dies on the earth exists for a time on the astral plane. In addition to these forms of life, with which we are more familiar, there are also countless myriads of other forms, some of which are called elementals, which have no counterpart on earth, but live wholly on the astral plane. These elementals have a certain amount of intelligence. Other astral entities have intelligence in different degrees. Some are malicious, some are cunning, some are mischievous, some harmless and mirthful. Any one of these creatures may find the opportunity to take control of an irresponsible medium. The lines of force permitting foreign control have been established in developing, and provide an open door, by which any astral entity may find it convenient to enter and manifest itself, even as an animal may walk into a house when the door is open.

Such entities are not above impersonation, and some are quite clever at it. Surely no one in his right mind can listen to the senseless drivel sometimes given forth by a medium in the trance state as coming from an intelligent loved one who has passed beyond, without realizing there is imposture. The mightiest intellects of the world are supposed by some to come back through mediums and utter time worn platitudes and inane remarks. They revel in the puerile and frivolous. Nor is the medium a fraud, he has merely been taken possession of by some astral entity who delights in perpetuating a hoax.

Yet because of such obvious untruthfulness and lack of integrity on the part of the entities that all too often control mediums we must not jump to the conclusion that all communications are unreliable, or that irresponsible mediums never really transmit messages from the dead. Sometimes the messages are genuine, and reveal beyond doubt the personality of the loved one. Sometimes the control is a departed friend who offers such proof of his identity that it can not be disputed. Particularly when the mediumship is developed and practiced in the sanctity of the home, and is accompanied by high spiritual ideals and noble desires is it more common to receive geniune communications from the dead. A pure heart and noble trend of mind do not tend to attract low or mischievous astral entities.

Sir Arthur Conan Doyle vouches for the following case of a spirit message which cannot be satisfactorily explained except as a genuine communication from the dead. He maintains that the circumstances were fully investigated and found to be quite authentic:

It seems in Australia the two sons of a couple interested in spiritualism had a boat in which they occasionally took a ride on the bay. On the particular day in question no one knew they were going boating, and no one saw them go. But at evening they failed to show up for dinner. Considerable concern was felt and after a time, when they failed still to appear, a seance was held. One of the youths took control of the medium and stated that a squall had upset their boat and that he had been devoured by a large fish which he described. No trace of the boys or the boat was found, but some days later a large shark, of a species which is almost never seen in those waters, drifted upon the beach, and in its stomach were found the watch and pocket knife of the boy who stated through the medium he had been devoured when the boat upset. The shark, a large blue one, if I remember correctly, also answered his description, being of great rarity in that region.

As no one knew the youths went boating, or knew that they upset, the information could not have been received telepathically from a living person. Besides, it would be beyond the power of any living person unless he was actually with the boys when the accident took place, to know what kind of a fish had devoured him, or that he had been eaten by a shark. Yet the description of this unusual fish was furnished.[1]

My very plain statement of the effects of irresponsible mediumship, based upon careful research and observations covering more than a quarter of a century and an intimate acquaintance with a great number of mediums, may seem quite discouraging to those who have hopes of communicating with their loved ones who have passed beyond the physical plane. But it need not be so, for I have so far only considered the negative, irresponsible and disintegra-

---

1. From a lecture given by Sir Arthur Conan Doyle at Trinity Auditorium, Los Angeles.

tive phases of mediumship. There is another form of mediumship that is positive, responsible, and constructive, by which it is possible, and without any injurious effects, to duplicate any phenomena that may be produced by the irresponsible and disintegrative method.

Tasting, smelling, seeing, hearing, and feeling are all forms of mediumship. Through direct contact with substances, or small portions of substances, the organs of taste, feeling, and smell have energy imparted to them that is transmitted by the nerves to the brain and thence through electromagnetic motions to the unconscious mind. Such mediumship does not depend upon negativeness and passivity, but upon the development of sensitive organs and upon the alertness that enables them to receive impressions from the outside world.

The faculty of clairvoyance[2] may be exercised with no more negativeness than it is necessary to exercise in the ordinary sense of sight. Transverse wave motions in space convey the image of an object to the eye. Through the optic nerve and brain the image is registered in the astral consciousness. Wave motions in the astral substance, corresponding to a transverse motion in space, convey the image of an astral object—and all physical objects have astral counterparts—to the organ of sight of the astral body. Through the astral eyes the image is registered upon the unconscious mind. When the image is raised into the region of consciousness the result

---

2. Book II, Ch. III and VI of Thirty Years of Psychical Research, by Richet, and Ch. VII of Death and Its Mystery, by Flammarion, are devoted to numerous authentic cases of clairvoyance.

is clairvoyance. Material objects offer no resistance to the passage of astral vibrations, hence by clairvoyance one may see what is transpiring on the opposite side of the earth, or in the homes of the dead. To do this requires the development of the ability to direct the astral sense of sight and the ability to raise from the astral brain the image so received into the physical brain. This is no more negative or disintegrative than is the exercise of memory, which it greatly resembles.

The old hermetic scientists classified telepathy[3] as the seventh sense, intuition being the sixth. It certainly presupposes a particular kind of sensitiveness by which the wave motions sent out through space by a person thinking may be intercepted and registered. It would seem, much as in a radio set, that the receiver must be able to tune in, or be keyed to a similar rate of vibration, in order to receive thought messages. Such ability does not depend upon negativeness, but upon sensitiveness or ability to extend consciousness. It is a faculty that may be cultivated without in any manner impairing self-control.

To hear another person speak it is not necessary that we subject our will to his. Neither is it necessary to be in any manner under the control of another in order to hear clairaudiently.[4] The astral body has organs of hearing, astral ears. Just as wave motions

3. For numerous authentic instances of telepathy, see Book III, Ch. II, of Thirty Years of Psychical Research, by Richet, and Ch. VI of Death and Its Mystery, by Flammarion.

4. For authentic cases of clairaudience see Thirty Years of Psychical Research, by Richet, p. 272, and After Death, by Flammarion, p. 91.

in the air carry sound to the physical ear, so other similar wave motions in astral substance carry astral sounds to the astral ear. The ability to hear clairaudiently may be cultivated much as the ability to hear physically may be cultivated, and exercised with no more injury.

To feel an object which we can touch necessitates a certain form of mediumship, but does not necessitate our being under some other entity's control. Everything has its astral counterpart, which retains as modes of motion the vibrations of its past and present environment. Through the astral sense of touch, called psychometry[5] these vibrations may be discerned, and their meaning may then be interpreted by the soul. This interpretation when raised into the region of consciousness may reveal all the events that have happened in the vicinity of the object. But this exercise of the psychometric faculty, while requiring alertness and the development of the ability to recognize the sense impressions of the astral body, needs no more irresponsible mediumship than does the physical sense of touch.

Prevision,[6] the seeing of that which is still in the future, is not dependent upon the disintegrative forms of mediumship. If one is so situated as to observe an aeronaut drop a sand bag from a balloon, he may predict to a friend standing in an adjoining room that in a few seconds a bag of sand will strike the earth at about a given spot. The friend, not see-

---

5. For authentic cases of psychometry see Thirty Years of Psyical Research by Richet, p. 188.
6. For numerous authentic cases of prevision see Thirty Years of Psychical Research, by Richet, Ch. VII, and Death and Its Mystery, by Flammarion, Ch. VIII and Ch. IX.

ing the balloon, may be quite startled at the fulfill-
ment of the prediction. Man's astral senses are able
to see the various factors converging which culminate
in an event.

It should be remembered that all that is ever experienced is retained in the unconscious mind, or
soul. This is proved both by hypnosis and by psychoanalysis. Under hypnosis a subject may be made to
recall any event of his past, events which are entirely
beyond his ability to remember in his normal waking
s t a t e.   Likewise, through the free association
method, the psychoanalyst causes his patient to remember events even in minute detail, which have
long been forgotten, and which ordinarily could not
have been recalled. Whatever man once knows he
never loses, for he retains it in his soul. Moreover,
what any man has ever known is never lost to the
human race, for the record is preserved as modes of
motion persisting in the astral world, and may be recovered by any person who can tune in on this record.

With such a storehouse of information to draw
from, in addition to the use of the psychic sense organs, previsions, remarkable as they often are, seem
less astounding.

These storehouses of knowledge are invariably
drawn upon by those whom the world calls geniuses.
Usually the genius is unaware of the source of his
knowledge and inspiration. Nevertheless a critical
comparison of the birth-charts of people who are
naturally psychic reveals that any person who has the
planet Neptune unusually prominent in his chart of

birth may develop the ability to contact and draw information, consciously or unconsciously, from the astral plane. Thomas A. Edison, the inventor, for instance, may or may not have faith in psychic matters, yet he has the Sun and Mercury in conjunction with Neptune, and all exceedingly strong by position, in his birth-chart. This makes it unusually easy for him, through extrasensory perception, to contact and draw information from the inner planes. In fact, of all the geniuses whose birth-charts I have examined up to the present time, I have so far found not one in which a prominent Neptune is absent. It would seem that every imaginable form of knowledge exists on the inner planes of life, and is accessible to those who can raise their vibrations sufficiently to tune in on it. Genius is the ability to contact such higher planes and assimilate the knowledge so received in such a manner as to be able to transmit it to less capable minds.

Not only do inanimate objects retain in their astral counterparts the impress of the events that transpire in their vicinity, but all organic material retains the mental impress of the life form that organized it. The desires and fears of an animal, for instance, are strongly implanted in the astral substance associated with its flesh. When man eats this flesh its astral vibrations tend to build up and fortify the animal nature within himself. If the animal was slain while in great pain or terror, this influence is incorporated into the astral counterpart of the flesh, and has a tendency to impart a similar vibration to the person eating it.

It is undoubtedly true that the original vibrations of the food one eats may be changed. Yet the food has had its astral vibrations polarized toward the soul of the form of which it was a portion, and so transmits more readily the grades of energy necessary for that form. Now man can obtain the proper chemical elements in organized form from widely different combinations of food. But while any balanced ration may supply him with blood and tissue and also transmit a grade of astral vibrations, still it is found he has greater difficulty in raising the tones to higher octaves of transmission with some foods than with others.

One of the laws of mediumship is that the grade of energy transmitted by anything depends upon the refinement of the substance. The more refined the instrument the higher and more potent the grade of energy that may be transmitted through it. Some foods have become so set in transmitting only the lower octaves of astral force that it is almost impossible to raise their vibrations to a point where they will transmit higher grades. At the same time these strongly polarized foods, such as the flesh of animals, while unaccustomed to transmitting finer forces, are capable of conveying even more readily those energies, which also are very useful in their proper place, that go to build up brute strength and physical force. The higher kinds of vegetable foods, not having been dominated by desires, not so strongly polarized, may more readily be converted into a medium for the transmission of those higher kinds of energy that nourish the intellect and soul powers.

From the laws of mediumship thus far mentioned it may be seen that life depends upon an organization capable of receiving and transmitting complex forms of energy, and the more refined the organization the higher the grade of energy transmitted and the higher the quality of life. Life, Light, and Love originate with God, and the amount of energy, intelligence, and affection any being expresses depends upon its ability to receive, utilize, and transmit some portion of these universal qualities.

In addition to pointing out the general laws of mediumship, I have been at some pains to explain the disintegrative effect of irresponsible mediumship. In the two following lessons I shall take up and explain the methods by which the various kinds of spiritistic and psychic phenomena are produced. But the student should not forget that any phenomena produced on the physical plane by a discarnate entity operating through a medium under control, might have been produced by the medium without such disintegrative control if he had undergone proper training.

Full instructions on the training necessary to produce such phenomena by the constructive method, and without being under the control of another, will be furnished the neophyte at the proper time. As to the methods by which the faculties of clairvoyance, telepathy, clairaudience, psychometry, and prevision may be developed along constructive lines, these are furnished without cost to all Church of Light members who demonstrate their fitness to use this knowledge by passing examinations on the B. of L. courses.

SPIRITISM

Serial No. 44

THE CHURCH OF LIGHT
Box 1525, Los Angeles 53, California

Printed in U.S.A.

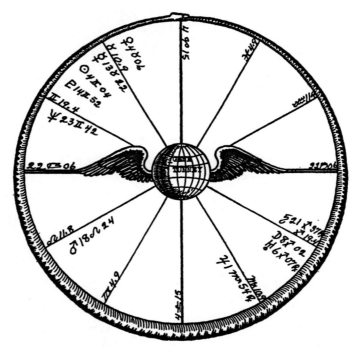

GENE TUNNEY, May 25, 1899, 8:00 a.m., 74W. 40:43N. Data given personally to Clement Hey.

1909, first boxing on tenth birthday: Mars sextile Neptune r.

1915, defeated in first professional fight: Sun sextile Mars r.

1917, March, injured elbow, atrophy set in: Sun opposition Saturn, r.

1919, took up boxing as career: Sun conjunction Neptune r, Venus square Mars p.

1926, knocked Dempsey out, became world champion: Sun trine Jupiter p, Mars square Sun r.

1927, again defeated Dempsey: Sun trine Jupiter p, Mars square Sun r; and in 1928 under these aspects retired champion of world.

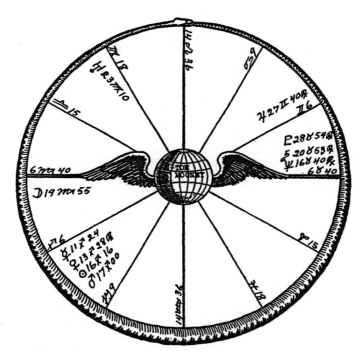

TOM MOONEY, December 8, 1882, 4:00 a.m., 87:50W. 42N.
Data furnished by his mother.

1913, alleged attempt to "frame" him: Sun trine Neptune *r*.

1916, July 22, arrested with four others in Preparedness Parade
bombing in which 10 were killed and 40 injured: Saturn opposition
Moon *r*, Sun trine Saturn *r*, M.C. trine Saturn *p*.

1917, February, verdict of guilty to be hanged; but labor move
started to free him on ground he was "framed." Movement lasted
over 20 years.

1938, January 7, unconditionally pardoned: Sun sextile Venus *r*,
Mercury trine Jupiter *p*.

SPIRITISM

AS IT IS now impossible for the well informed person to doubt the reality of a wide variety of psychic phenomena, there is an increasing demand for their rational explanation. I propose, therefore, to take up, one after another the various types of such phenomena, and elucidate them according to the doctrines of Hermetic Science.

Before doing this, however, it may be well to mention a few of the numerous other ways in which mediumship plays a part in human life.

It has already been mentioned that the active always controls the passive, and that the grade of energy transmitted by anything depends upon its refinement. A water pipe transmits a flow of water because it has a structure suited to such transmission. A copper wire, on the other hand, because of difference in composition and form, will not transmit water, but is a medium for the ready transmission of electricity. A coarse-textured man, because his nervous system and brain are coarser in structure, transmits a grosser form of emotional and sensational energy, and consequently enjoys a form of recreation quite repugnant to the fine-skinned, fine-haired, more sensitive person. The finer the structure and the more highly organized it is, the finer the quality of energy that may pass through it.

In man we find the climax of physical evolution. In his brain and nervous system there is greater refinement and a higher organization than in any other mundane form. As a consequence, man is able to re-

ceive and transmit more subtle energies than lower
forms of life.

Man a microcosm.—His physical body is the product of evolution, as the many vestigal structures present in it clearly prove. Embryology also points this
out in no uncertain terms, for the human embryo, as
do all embryos, briefly recapitulates the history of
its ancestry. The life forms through which it has developed are shown in the forming child. In addition
to such a physical history, man also contains within
himself the history of his soul's evolution through
lower life forms. The various traits of character,
the impulses and desires, present in lower forms of
life, are all present in man, as psychoanalysis plainly
reveals. But for the most part they have been developed, transformed, and sublimated, into something higher and more beautiful. Nevertheless, in
man are the vestiges, both of the structures and the
tendencies, of innumerable other and lower forms
of life.

It is further true, as a study of natal astrology
demonstrates, that man has within himself in miniature all that is in the heavens above. The zodiacal
signs and the planets, as well as other celestial bodies,
have their correspondences within his constitution.
When they move they produce discernible changes in
man. When they form definite relations to each other,
called aspects, man feels differently than he did when
such aspects were not formed, and unless he under-
stands the source of his impulses, he may act in response to these feelings.

Because man has within himself something corresponding to all that is below him in the scale of evolu-

tion, and correspondences to all in the sky above, and also, it is to be inferred, to all forms of intelligences above him in the evolutionary scale, the ancient Hermetics called man a microcosm. This means that man may be considered a universe in miniature.

Man a transformer of energy.—As a microcosm, or little universe, man is able to receive and transmit a very wide variety of energies. In addition to the energy derived from the food he eats and the air he breathes, he is also the medium for countless other forces.

His astral body constantly receives and transmits the energy radiated by the planets. Even as the sun acts as a transformer for the high-frequency energies of space, so man in his turn acts as a transformer of planetary energies. He is also a transmitter of intellectual and spiritual energies that reach him as wave motions from regions of greater intelligence and spirituality. The grade of intellectual and spiritual force he transmits depends upon his mental development and soul unfoldment.

The astral energies radiated by the planets are intercepted by his astral body, being received more freely at those points in his astral structure, as indicated by planets in his birth-chart, that were organized by states of consciousness previous to his birth. These astral energies are even more essential to the welfare of the astral body than is sunlight to the welfare of the physical body. Only a portion of such energies received, however, is utilized by the person. The balance undergoes transformation, or change in frequency of vibration, and is again radiated, much as the sun and planets receive energy of a more general character and giving it a special trend radiate it again.

Likewise, such spiritual and intellectual energy as man receives or generates is again in large measure radiated. As seen by clairvoyant vision this radiation is of two distinct and separate qualities. The more gross astral energies and thought vibrations flow forth to remain in contact with the earth, and may be received in measure by lower life forms. In other words, the thoughts and feelings of man, as well as certain other astral energies, flow about and permeate the earth, so that other life forms coming in contact with them may receive and appropriate such of them as their organization will permit. In the upward struggle of the seven sub-mundane degrees of life, this force radiated by man and penetrating to the very center of the earth, is of great assistance. It affords these degrees of life from mineral to man whatever of intellectual energies they are capable of absorbing and utilizing. It thus hastens their evolution through providing them with mental nutriment and the incentive to effort.

The other and more spiritual portion of the force radiated by man travels away from the earth and the astral plane immediately surrounding it. There are seven super-mundane realms of life; realms of life whose denizens have never been, and never will be, incarnated on earth. They form a gradation in spirituality of seven steps between man and the angel. Being too spiritual and lacking in penetrative and initiative force for incarnation in gross matter, they depend upon man for all knowledge of material conditions. The higher essences of man's intellectual and spiritual endeavors may be assimilated by them and give them information that is a requisite of their progress.

But now I must return to earth, and to matters that are susceptible of proof by the average man.

Action of mind at a distance.—A very common phenomenon, and one that should be understood by everyone so that all may avoid becoming the dupes of unscrupulous practical psychologists, is the exercise of thought power to influence another person's thoughts and actions without the intervention of the spoken word or any sign.

It is possible, for instance, in a public gathering, to concentrate the mind on some person and make him turn and look at one. If the person is known to the experimenter it will be much easier thus to influence him, for a point of contact will previously have been established. But it is possible thus to influence a total stranger. Such experiments which have been rigidly tested out and after coincidence has been eliminated found actually to produce the desired effect, are very simple, but they demonstrate in a very forcible and convenient way that the mind of one person can, and sometimes does, influence another person at a distance.

Further, it is not uncommon for a hypnotist to direct the actions of his subject by mental command alone. There is plenty of irrefutable evidence that this has been successfully done.[1] The various kinds of absent treatments applied by metaphysicians, mental scientists, christian scientists, and new thought practitioners, are practical applications of this power of one person to influence another at a distance.

The thought of one individual sets up lines of force in astral substance which reach the second individual, and if the experiment is successful, sets up vibrations similar to the thought held, in the unconscious mind or astral body of the other individual. If the person to whom the thought is sent is one who is in the habit of controlling his own thoughts and actions his unconscious mind will repel, and will not accept the thought sent to it, unless it is a thought quite acceptable and perceived to be for his welfare. But if the person has cultivated irresponsible mediumship, or is naturally negative, the thought will enter the unconscious mind and may quite dominate it. The thoughts and actions then will be those willed by the person sending the thought.

No person who habitually controls his own thoughts and actions need be dominated by any other person or entity.[2] The soul that has built the body about itself, under normal circumstances is quite able to resist foreign invasion from any source. It is aware that to turn around and look at someone who is concentrating on it in a public meeting is not apt to prove detrimental, but it will resist detrimental mental commands even as it would resist them if they were uttered aloud.

Power of thought to change bodily form.—Once a thought image has been accepted, however, particularly if the image be strong and vivid, momentous results may follow. The physical body is shaped and moulded by the astral body. Normally this moulding is quite gradual, but when the image in the uncon-

1. Death and Its Mystery, by Flammarion, ch. V.
2. Explicit instructions for protecting oneself from the mental influence of another are given in Lesson No. 101.

scious mind is supported by an unusual amount of energy it brings about such a radical and abrupt change in the astral form that the physical also is drastically transformed. In proof of this, it would be an easy matter to cite numerous instances in which persons have been instantly healed by mental or spiritual treatment, such healing being accompanied by marked changes in the body and its functions. Almost everyone nowadays knows of one or more such cases.

Stigmata.—But this power of the mind, acting through imagination upon the astral body, to make radical changes in the physical, is even more dramatically exemplified in numerous cases of stigmata. Stigmata is the receiving upon the body, through religious devotion, wounds similar to those of which the Nazarene died on the cross. Holes are formed in the palms of the hands and on the soles of the feet, and the side opens as if it had been pierced by a spear. Blood actually flows from these holes, and also often from wounds on the forehead where the Nazarene wore His crown of thorns, being caused solely through the action of the mind.

Saint Francis of Assisi received such stigmata. Yet as he lived so long ago, materialists put the whole matter down as a legend. But cases of stigmata also occur at the present day, and have been thoroughly investigated by competent scientists. The verdict is that stigmata do actually occur, and that they emit blood.[1].

Speaking in strange tongues.—Before leaving the subject of the power of one mind to influence another at a distance, it is well worth recording that a command given in a language that the person influenced does not understand has almost as much force as if given in his own language. His unconscious mind, having much keener perceptions than his objective mind, recognizes the thought behind the words, and tends to be influenced by this thought.[1]

From this ability of the unconscious mind to recognize the import of words of a strange language, to speaking in strange tongues, is but a step. There is no doubt now of the ability of many persons when more or less under the control of a hypnotist or astral entity, to talk intelligently in a language with which they are normally unfamiliar. Such ability is reported to have been common among the saints and early Christian fathers. By certain religious sects at the present day, talking in strange tongues and the ability to heal by laying on of the hands is required of those who claim to have received grace in full measure. To be sure, in many instances this strange speech is unintelligible, but at other times it is really recognizable talk.

In these cases, as in the cases of the saints of old who often had aureoles about their heads, appeared simultaneously in more than one locality, possessed an "odour of sanctity," had the faculty of prophecy, suffered levitation, and were insensible to fire; it is difficult to determine just how much of the phenomena is produced by the activity of their own unconscious minds and how much is due to the control exercised over them by discarnate entities. In cases of speaking in tongues at religious conversions, I believe, from my own observations, that a high percentage in their emotional frenzy become dominated

---

1. Death and Its Mystery, by Frammarion, ch. V.

and controlled by astral entities of some kind.

The ouija board.—One of the most familiar approaches to psychic phenomena is by way of the ouija board or planchette. Particularly since the war, during which so many gallant sons and fathers laid down their lives, has the ouija board come into vogue. Little wonder, when the craving is so strong to again converse with loved ones from whom violently parted.

The ouija board and planchette consist of either a flat board or a dial upon which are printed letters, numbers, and perhaps a few useful words. There is a movable pointer so arranged that it may easily be moved over the board in such a manner as to point to the characters on the board or dial. This pointer is of such size that one or several persons may rest their finger tips gently upon it.

In operating the ouija board — and the planchette works practically the same — the most approved method is to place the board upon the laps of two persons, preferably a lady and a gentleman. The fingers of both are placed lightly but firmly upon the small table which acts as a pointer, this table being on the board and permitted to move freely over it. In a few minutes this small table commences to move; at first slowly, and then with more speed. Thus it is able to talk by touching the letters and characters printed on the board, and if questions are asked it will answer them.

In using the ouija board and similar appliances, the more negative and passive the experimenters, as a rule, the more satisfactory the results. The questions may be asked either orally or mentally and are answered with equal success.

Now, most of the motions made by man are not the result of premeditated thought, but are directed by the unconscious mind. To be sure, we think of walking and then walk. But walking is a very elaborate and intricate process of balancing the action of one muscle against another. That is, the nervous system has been educated to respond with the utmost alacrity to commands issued by the unconscious mind.

Because of the facility with which the unconscious mind can cause unconscious muscular actions, it is easier, in the normal run of things, for the unconscious mind to communicate intelligent thoughts through directing appropriate muscular actions than for it to impress the thoughts directly upon the physical brain. Hence it is that the use of unconscious muscular activity is the easiest method possible, under ordinary circumstances, for communicating that which is in the unconscious mind to the cognition of the physical brain. It is due to this that more people can get psychic messages through the ouija board and such devices than through any other method.

Range of information of the soul.—As has been pointed out in the last lesson, the field of information accessible to the unconscious mind is enormously greater than that open to the physical consciousness. All that the person has ever experienced or known is stored up in the unconscious mind. The range of the astral perceptions is infinitely greater than those of the physical senses. It may tune in on almost any imaginable source of information, not only on the record preserved in the astral world of all that man has known and thought, but it may also come mentally in touch with still higher centers of information.

Therefore, the questions that the soul of a person using the ouija board may answer intelligently are exceedingly wide in scope. And undoubtedly it is commonly the case that a portion of the information given through the ouija board emanates from the experimenter's unconscious mind.

While such a range of perception and such a storehouse of knowledge may be used by the unconscious mind, it is probable, because the unconscious mind requires much training to utilize a very extensive range, that in many cases a large part of the information received through the ouija board comes from some discarnate entity. This is all the more certain because the astral world about and interpenetrating the earth is so crowded with astral entities who seem to have no objection whatever to taking control of a negative person and manifesting through him whatever of intelligence, or lack of it, they possess.

Another factor influencing the veracity of psychic communications of all kinds is the susceptibility of the unconscious mind to suggestion. It has been educated to obey the desires of the objective mind. Therefore, if there is a strong desire for a certain type of manifestation, and no controlling entity is present, it quite naturally endeavors of itself to produce the phenomena. If there is a strong desire present on the part of the experimenter to receive a message of a certain kind, or on the part of other persons present, which it is able to perceive, it will try to deliver such a message as is wanted. The message but reflects the desire of someone present, and may be widely at variance with the truth. And even though some other entity is in control and trying to give a truthful and important message, the unconscious mind, under the influence of the desires of those present, may still have power enough to warp the message out of all semblance to its original self. Truthful, serious messages may be expected only when those present are serious, and above all else, desire the truth, however discomforting it may be.

Factors influencing veracity of spirit messages.— We now perceive that in all spirit messages there are three factors which may be present in widely varying proportions, and which may have an influence upon the message. There is the unconscious mind of the medium, which may be entirely responsible for the message, or which may have almost nothing whatever to do with it. There is the desire and combined thought force of those present acting upon the subconscious mind of the medium. This may amount to almost nothing in some instances, and in others may be the deciding element. Then there is the presence of one or more astral entities, which may be intelligent or may be ignorant, which may be impersonations and hoaxes, or may be as they represent themselves to be. They may have but partial control of the medium and not be responsible for the message, or they may be in complete control and the sole authors of it. The self-controlled clairvoyant can see these entities and can feel whether or not they are genuine or are wearing a mask of deception, but the irresponsible medium has no way of knowing whether or not his controls are as represented.

Proof of Human Survival.—Undoubtedly those who have once lived on the earth and passed to the next realm sometimes communicate with those yet in the flesh through such simple devices as the ouija board. Ouija-board answers usually are trivial and shallow, or but shadow the thoughts of those present. Yet occasionally information is thus received of astounding correctness and great value. Instances are recorded in which such messages have saved lives, and other instances in which information was received known to no living person. People who have disappeared leaving no trace, drowned without witnesses, have been able to communicate the method of their death and direct searchers to the physical remains.

There are other cases recorded where people have been directed to dig for mineral deposits where there were no surface indications; consequently the location could have been known to no living person, and the mineral deposits so located have proven of great value. These are exceptional cases, it is true, and many a poor dupe has been sent to dig for mineral where there was none. Yet these successful cases can not be accounted for by the theory that the knowledge was transmitted from the mind of some living person. Undoubtedly, as I said, under certain circumstances those physically dead communicate again with the living.

The range of power of the unconscious mind of living man is so extensive that it taxes human ingenuity to the utmost to devise any test by which human survival may be proved. One of the tests, recently devised, called cross-correspondences, is meeting with considerable success. The discarnate personality, through several widely separated mediums, gives fragments of classical quotations, or other matters with which he was familiar when on earth, and of which the mediums are quite ignorant. These fragmentary messages, having no meaning separately, are directed to be sent to the Psychical Research Society, where they are pieced together, and not only make sense, but reveal something that research shows the person giving the message was familiar with, and would naturally use to establish his identity. These experiments are yet in their infancy, yet even so far as they have been carried, they seem to me to establish the survival of the human personality beyond a reasonable doubt.

In these communications which we have been considering, the medium is more or less under control. I shall not violently condemn the use of the ouija board. It does imply, however, loss of control of the body and mind in small degree. In just so far as there is success with the ouija board, precisely so much has disintegrative and irresponsible mediumship been established. Some force other than the normal personality has usurped the power temporarily to use a portion of the astral brain, nervous system, and muscles. It is so much lost in the struggle to command the body and progress in evolution. Yet a few raindrops do not make a river, nor do a few drinks made a drunkard. Many people believe that strong liquor in moderation is more beneficial than the reverse. They admit that excess is ruinous, but contend that the pleasure to be derived from drinking within limits is greater than the harm done the body by the alcohol.

Such persons could with equal logic extend their argument to the use of the ouija board. At least it seems to be the least harmful of negative mediumistic endeavors. As a rule the amount of control is small. And while I know of a few persons who have gone to excess with the ouija board and landed in the psychopathic ward, as also I know certain drunkards who once believed they could "drink or leave it alone," yet I also know hundreds of people who have experimented with the ouija board, and even with automatic writing, which requires a stronger extraneous control, who, from all appearances, are none the worse for it.

Wise spiritual intelligences use impression.—Of this, however, I am quite positive; truly wise spiritual intelligences do not make a practice of communicating through a person under control. In dire necessity, on some rare occasion, they may do so, but only because no other avenue is available and the message must be given.

Wise spiritual intelligences, when they are permitted to do so, give their messages by impression. Aware of the disintegrative effect upon the medium of controlling him, they refuse to exercise such control. They merely talk forcefully to the astral counterpart of the person they wish to impress. The astral body is not controlled, but has full knowledge of what is being said and who is saying it. It is a matter of conversation, not always one sided, even as two people ordinarily talk on meeting. This communication, which is given by an astral person—a disembodied person—to the astral counterpart of a person still in the flesh, rises from the unconscious mind into the region of objective consciousness. It may seem, if the person is not accustomed to receiving such impressions, but a vague realization that a certain thing is a fact. If the person receiving the message is a little more advanced in psychic matters, it may rise into objective consciousness as a series of complete and precise sentences, but with no very clear knowledge of the source from which derived. But if the receiver has practiced to develop the ability, he may be as fully aware of who is talking and what is being said as if he were talking to a friend in the flesh.

A great deal of information, and I am sorry to say misinformation also, is given by those of the inner planes to those on the outer plane who delve into occult matters, without the recipient being aware of the source from which his impressions come. He merely feels that something is true, or all at once some information flashes into his mind. I speak of misinformation advisedly, for those who pass to the next plane of life do not immediately become all wise. Until educated away from them, which may be a very long time for one who on earth was very set in his ideas, they still hold to the same beliefs and habits of thought that they held on earth. They may be quite as much in error, and quite as dogmatic about it, as anyone in the world. Only those who keep an open mind and endeavor to learn the unprejudiced truth make rapid progress on the inner planes toward a better understanding of truth than those on earth. And these, invariably, when they find a seeker who is worthy, endeavor to impress him with a knowledge of truth as they have found it. Hence the oft repeated slogan in occult circles that whenever the neophyte is ready, behold, the master appears. But a master teaches, admonishes, and advises his chosen pupil, the same as he would do if he were a spirit in the flesh. No true master places his neophyte, or anyone else, under control.

It is always a joy to the scholarly men of earth to find someone with a desire to emulate them in the acquirement of knowledge. As I know from observation and experience, those who master difficult branches of learning are ever eager to help the younger student who aspires to acquaint himself in the same branch. And when they find a pupil who shows considerable ability they go to great pains to help him over the difficult parts of the road.

This is quite as true of wise spiritual intelligences. They are always eager to find a pupil who is worthy of instruction. Yet they are not desirous of shouldering all his responsibilities in life, or of advising him on every trivial matter. Each soul should cultivate his individuality and learn to decide his own issues whenever possible. But wise spiritual beings are ever ready to advise us if we indicate by our efforts and aspirations that we are striving to help ourselves. This they do through impression.

Automatic writing.—Next to the ouija board in popularity is automatic writing. The medium sits at a table with a sheet of paper before him. He grasps a pencil in his hand and places his hand in the position of one writing. He then becomes passive and awaits results. When the controlling entity has succeeded in establishing rapport with the sitter—which really consists of organizing such lines of force between its astral form and the astral form of the sitter that it can communicate its own motions to the form of the subject—the hand begins to write through no volitional effort of the medium, and usually the medium is ignorant of what is being written.

Rapport.—Before going further I should explain more about rapport. Both those in the flesh and those out of the flesh can raise and lower their vibrations temporarily to a certain extent, much as the strings of a musical instrument can be changed in tension. To communicate rates of motion from one entity to another requires only that some of the vibrations of their astral bodies have similar frequencies. This forms a point of contact through which the more active can inject its rates of motion if the frequencies are made synchronous—that is, vibrate in unison, the crest of a wave motion in one corresponding in point of time to the crest of a wave motion in the other. Synchronism is easy when one of the entities becomes passive.

The active entity, once a point of contact is established, injects more and more of its rates of motion into the astral body of the medium. The vibrations of the medium are thus raised or lowered until they very largely vibrate in unison to those of the controlling entity. The entity then has complete control and the medium is powerless.

Rapport is established when the vibrations of one entity vibrate in unison with those of another entity. Rapport does not imply control, for two persons may be in rapport and neither exercise control of the other. Rapport merely facilitates the exchange of energy, and may be the result of similar rates of energy present due to similar thoughts and similar planetary influences at birth, or it may be produced artificially by raising or lowering the vibrations. Rapport is very important and valuable, but in the case of negative mediumship it is a principle used by the controlling entity for obtaining controlling of the medium. Once control is gained, the more thorough the rapport the fuller the control.

The astral world is so crowded with entities of different grades and kinds that a call sent out by a medium for a control is quite sure to be answered by something. It may even be answered by the deceased personality who is supposed to be in control. But however the message may be communicated through an irresponsible medium; whether by the ouija board, automatic writing, table tipping, the control of the medium's vocal organs, or in some other fashion; in addition to the probability of some entity exercising control of the medium's body, there is also a possibility that the message emanates from, or at least is colored by, the unconscious mind of the medium or the thoughts, conscious and subconscious, of those present.

In automatic writing the controlling entity, after establishing rapport with the medium, is able to direct the arm and hand in writing whatever it may desire.

Table-tipping.—In table-tipping[3] unconscious muscular contractions, such as are used in ouija-board communications and automatic writing, are made use of to start with, but there soon develops an additional factor. Those present sit in a circle about a small table, placing their finger tips lightly upon it. Soon the table begins to vibrate distinctly, and when

3. For authentic examples see Thirty Years of Psychical Research, by Richet, p. 401.

this vibration reaches a certain tension the table begins to move about in a more or less intelligent manner.

It is truly wonderful what power of expression can manifest through a small wooden table. It often moves toward one of the sitters and actually caresses him, or it may manifest enmity through violent gyrations. Someone present asks the table if the control is a certain person long dead, and when the right name is mentioned the table pounds violently on the floor. It answers questions by pounding on the floor or rocking violently to express an affirmative, and slows almost to a stop to express a negative reply. It also communicates by a prearranged code, tapping on the floor, or moving in a certain manner to make itself understood.

The additional factors, of which I made mention, are the electromagnetic emanations of those present, which are used by the control to set the table vibrating and to assist in its movements. The control, through its rapport, or close association with the astral form of the medium, is able to communicate motions set up by it in astral substance to these electromagnetic forces drawn from the sitters. This electromagnetic force may then be directed through the table and its motions imparted to the physical substance of the table.

The use of electromagnetic energy drawn from organic substance, and in the case of table-tipping drawn from the medium and others present, seems to be an absolute requisite for the exerting of physical force by a discarnate entity. Another rule, while perhaps not absolute, yet at least of common observance, is that the more physical force exerted by a discarnate entity the less intelligence it manifests. Clairvoyants and seers of all ages claim that strong physical manifestations of psychic force are nearly always produced by entities low in intelligence, chiefly elementals, but who possess much strength in the lower astral currents. It is truly surprising how many mediums who do healing or produce physical phenomena claim American Indians as controls. They hold that the Indians are closer to the earth and consequently have more power to give strong physical manifestations.

In table-tipping the particles of the table become so charged with energy as to give the impression of being alive. Anyone who has had experience with genuine table-tipping could not be deceived as to whether or not there is a strong psychic influence present, for there is a peculiar vibration in the wood that may be distinctly felt before, and as, the table begins to move. Not infrequently, also, the table is levitated completely from the floor, or continues to rock, while no fingers are closer than several inches above it, and on occasions it moves entirely across the room with no one touching it.

Levitation.—This brings us to the subject of levitation.[4] The movement of light objects, and also the movement of heavy objects, at a distance from the medium, sometimes at a great distance, and without physical contact of any kind, has been thoroughly established by men of international scientific reputation. Chairs, tables, and many other objects, includ-

---

4. Abundant authentic instances of levitation are given in Thirty Years of Psychical Research, by Richet, p. 421.

ing sometimes the medium, are lifted into the air and suspended there without visible means of support.

The late Mr. W. J. Crawford, D.Sc., lecturer in engineering at the Municipal Technical Institute, Belfast, by a great number of experiments, established, through placing the medium on a weighing machine, that it is customary for the medium to gain in weight as much as the object lifted; also, that when an object is made heavier than normal, the medium, though at a distance, loses in weight the amount gained by the object. This leads to the conclusion that there is an invisible astral and electromagnetic connection between the medium and the object acted upon. The controlling entity extends the medium's astral body, and this becomes the moulding power by which electromagnetic emanations present are used as energy to lift the distant object or to hold it down. It is as if an invisible and extremely elastic arm reached out from the medium to act upon the physical object.

Other experiments indicate that it is quite common where objects are lifted or moved by invisible forces, for each of the persons present, some more and some less, to contribute to the moving force. Each person in the circle may gain something in weight when a heavy object like an oak table or a piano is lifted from the floor by an invisible force. The controlling entity is able not only to use the electromagnetic emanations of the medium, but also to use extensions from the astral bodies and the electromagnetic energies of every person present, in more or less degree, in the lifting of material objects. If a sudden shock disturbs the medium, the object will drop to the floor, because the communicating lines of force between the medium and the object have been broken.

It would be stating more than has been proved, and more than is probable, to say that objects are only levitated by pressure exerted by an extension of the medium's astral and electromagnetic bodies. In certain cases of hauntings, which will be discussed in the next lesson, objects apparently move when there is no human medium near, and irrespective of whether or not there are witnesses. It is not uncommon for pictures to be violently thrown from the wall, clocks to stop, raps, knocks, and other physical manifestations to take place at the moment of death of a relative in a distant land.[5] The dying person may act through the astral body and electromagnetic emanations of some person in the house where the manifestations take place, may use the electromagnetic emanations drawn from his own body, or in rarer instances there may be electromagnetic energy associated with the physical substance of the environment that is available. It seems that it is not always essential for the production of physical phenomena to have a human being to draw upon, but such human is at least present in by far the majority of cases. Certainly, in all cases, there is present an available supply of electromagnetic energy that has been associated with organic life.

If we bear in mind the way in which an extension of a medium's astral body is able to act as a lever to lift objects at a distance, we at once see how an extension of the medium's astral body, which is able to

5. For authentic instances see At The Moment of Death, by Flammarion, ch. IX.

assume any desired form, may hold the medium to the floor. In this way, certain mediums are able to increase their weight at will, although of course, being in a trance state, they know nothing about how the effect is produced.

Spirit rappings.—We also now are able to perceive how spirit raps[6] and knocks are produced. These noises in the home of the Fox sisters were the commencement of modern spiritualism. They may occur on a table, on the walls, on the ceiling, or apparently even from the air overhead. When the raps seem to come from a wall or solid object, the wall or object vibrates as if it had received a blow. An invisible projection from the medium sufficiently strong to lift a chair or table, it seems to me, should experience little difficulty in striking a blow that can be heard, or in producing condensation and sudden expansion of the air in limited areas to produce an explosive effect. But in all these cases the noises are, as I believe, produced through electromagnetic motions organized by astral lines of force from the medium, to such a consistency as to be able to communicate motion to physical substance.

Slate writing.—Slate writing and direct writing[7] are doubtless produced by extensions of the medium's astral body being used by the controlling entity to establish lines of electromagnetic energy sufficiently strong to write messages with a pencil. Slate writing is usually accomplished by placing a bit of slate pencil between two slates, that have been washed clean,

6. For authentic instances see Thirty Years of Psychical Research, by Richet, p. 443.
7. For authentic instances see Thirty Years of Psychical Research, by Richet, p. 448.

locking the slates together, and giving them to the medium or to some person present to hold. In a few minutes the noise of writing is heard on the inside of the slates, and after a rap is given by the entity as a signal that the work is finished, the slates are opened and found to contain a message signed by some deceased person.

Other writing is produced on blank sheets of paper on which have been placed bits of lead pencil.

Precipitation.—Still another phase of writing is known as precipitation. Cases are on record where blank sheets of paper have been covered with writing, voluminous MSS. containing information unknown to the medium, being so received in a short time. Beautiful pictures also sometimes appear on slates or upon paper in the same manner.

The rapidity with which such writing and such pictures are produced leads to the belief that the controlling entity is able to visualize clearly a whole picture, or a whole page of writing, and to transfer bits of pencil, or the various pigments, to the slate or page almost at once. That matter may be made to pass through matter was first demonstrated by Prof. Zollner and set forth in his book, "Transcendental Physics." The experiments with materializations, to be discussed in the next lesson, indicate that dematerialization of matter sometimes takes place. The bits of pencil used in precipitated writings, and the pigments used in precipitated pictures, may be materialized from non-material substance, or they may be produced by collecting the minute particles of all substances that exist in the air. But more likely they are derived from existing pencils and pigments and are transported to the place where precipitated in a dematerialized state, to assume the normal physical form again when precipitated as writing or as a picture.

In these cases also, the controlling entity undoubtedly uses the astral body and electromagnetic emanations of the medium. It uses them to build such lines of force as will collect and precipitate the proper materials in the form it has visualized.

Extrasensory perception.—The discovery of Pluto, the inner-plane planet and the planet of statistics and mass production, early in 1930, was immediately followed by the application of experimental methods and statistics to the investigation of telepathy, clairvoyance and precognition by a dozen universities, encouraged by the work of Dr. J. B. Rhine at Duke University. The university scientists now group these and allied faculties of the soul under the one term, extra-sensory perception, usually designated merely as ESP.

Dr. Rhine published his monograph, "Extra-Sensory Perception," in 1934; Stuart and Pratt published, "Handbook for Testing Extra-Sensory Perception," and Rhine published, "New Frontiers of the Mind," in 1937; and in 1940 Rhine, Pratt, Greenwood, Smith and Stuart collaborated in publishing, "Extra-Sensory Perception After Sixty Years." The painstaking work of these men, and that of other university experimenters, not only conclusively prove that man possesses ability to gain information by telepathy and clairvoyance, but that almost as easily it is possible to gain information of the future, termed by them precognition.

Also coincident with the discovery of Pluto, university scientists began to accept, and use in teaching physics, Einstein's Special Theory of Relativity. This acceptance is now practically universal.

Relativity holds that time and velocity are always interrelated, that physical velocities cannot exceed that of light, that anything moving with the velocity of light no longer possesses length, has infinite mass, and for it time has come to a standstill. Yet in the region where the soul chiefly functions, on the inner plane, or astral world, velocities are greater than those of light, and there consequently is a different order of gravitation, a different order of distance, and a different order of time.

This slower time of the inner plane enables us in a logical manner to account for both postcognition and precognition: Seeing something as it existed at some particular instance in the past or as it will probably appear at some particular instant in the future; which the university scientists prove man sometimes actually does. When we move our consciousness to the inner plane—the realm in which life normally functions after physical death—where velocities are greater than those of light, an infinite number of events can be condensed into one moment of this stand-still time and we are able to see backward and forward along the time-flow of external life and observe or have in one moment, experiences which in the rapid time of external life would occupy days, months or even years.

Relativity also makes clear why the inner-plane high-velocity, slow-time region cannot exchange energies with the low-velocity, fast-time region of out-

er-plane existence directly, but that all contact between the two must be made through Boundary-Line
electromagnetic energies which have approximately
the velocity of light. The various relations of inner-
plane existence and outer-plane existence are set
forth in full detail in lessons Nos. 14, 16, 18, 118
and Course XX, The Next Life.

Seance rooms.—Now, before closing this lesson, as
I have repeatedly referred to irresponsible mediums
and their seances, I should perhaps give a certain
warning to the less experienced about seance rooms.
Every person should, it seems to me, avail himself,
if the opportunity arises, of seeing some genuine
psychic phenomena. People of a scientific turn of
mind and positive makeup can investigate mediums
with impunity. Persons less positive readily become
influenced by astral entities if they attend seances,
it is particularly true if they attend developing circles.

It is quite common for the entities controlling the
medium to use the astral and electromagnetic energies of the medium to crush any resistance offered to
their control of other persons present. They also use
these energies to form a point of contact with persons present, following them home and endeavoring
to make the contact permanent and take full control.
If such a person is mediumistic or sensitive, the astral
entities may gain a power of influence, even though
the person is unaware of it. Such a person, if no
more serious influence is experienced, gets the seance
habit, and runs to a medium for advice on every
trivial occasion. He becomes a seance addict. The
seance room, while it serves a useful scientific purpose, is not without its dangers.

PHENOMENAL SPIRITISM

45

THE CHURCH OF LIGHT
Box 1525, Los Angeles 53, California

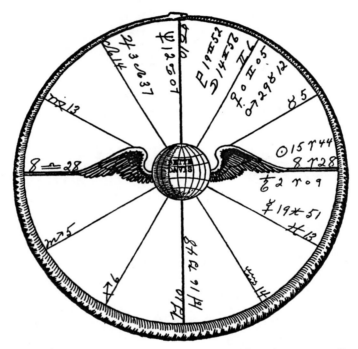

BETTE DAVIS, April 5, 1908, 5:33 p. m. (time given personally by her was evening). 71:15 W. 42:40N.

1930, December, after stage career, entered movies: Jupiter trine Saturn *p*, Mars conjunction Moon *r*, Moon square Neptune *r* (movies).

1935, won Academy Award by performance in "Dangerous": Sun sextile Neptune *r* in house of honor (tenth).

1938, again won Academy Award: Sun semi-sextile Moon *r*.

1938, became president of Tailwaggers Guide-Dog Institute: Mars square Mercury *r* in house of dogs (sixth).

1938, was granted divorce: Mars, co-ruler of husband (seventh), conjunction Pluto *r* and square Mercury *r*.

1942, was instrumental in starting Hollywood Canteen for service men and women: Sun sextile Mercury *r* in house of soldiers (sixth.)

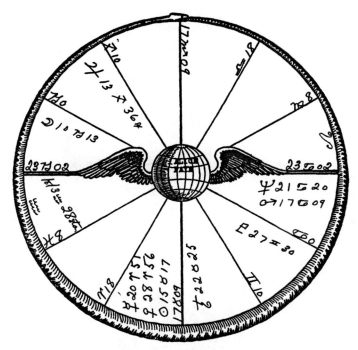

ALICE FAYE, May 5, 1912, midnight, 74W. 40:43N. Data given by Sid Skolsky in The Hollywood Citizen.

1931, was "discovered" by Rudy Vallee, who gave her big chance singing in his famous band: Sun trine Uranus r.

1934, began working in the movies: Sun semi-square Neptune r (movies), Mercury conjunction Sun r.

1935, first big movie success: Venus semi-sextile Pluto r in fifth (entertainment), Mercury sextile Mars r.

1937, September 4, married band leader Tony Martin: Sun opposition Jupiter p.

1939, career conflicts between herself and husband resulted in divorce: Mars, co-ruler of career (tenth), opposition Uranus r.

For years continued a success in the movies, married again and had several children.

PHENOMENAL SPIRITISM

BEFORE discussing the weird subject of haunted houses, and the astounding discoveries recently made in regard to materializations, it will probably be best first to explain certain phenomena of more common experience.

Among these, and having occurred to some member of almost every family at some time, are monitions. Monitions differ from premonitions in that while they denote a recognition of some event or condition that could not be known by the normal faculties, they do not anticipate future events.

These monitions generally occur at the time of an accident to an acquaintance, at the time of the illness of some person not present, or at the time of some absent person's death. But sometimes they occur concerning trivial matters. They occur to persons who are not generally regarded as unusually sensitive, and who, perhaps, have had no other such experience in their lives.

More commonly there are no objective phenomena. The person receiving the monition sees the image of a distant friend, or hears the friend calling him, or hears a loud knock on the wall, or has a dream in which he sees the friend dying or meeting with an accident. Later the news comes that the friend actually has died, or has had an accident. Thousands of people have had such experiences, and there is a multitude of authentic cases on record.[1]

Premonitions.— Premonitions, also, are of everyday experience. There are numerous authentic records[2] in which, without knowing a certain person is
approaching, and perhaps not having seen him for a
long time, other persons will commence to talk about
him, and be very much surprised when he puts in an
appearance. At times someone will see the phantasm
of the approaching person so plainly for a moment
as to think it an objective reality, and believe he
actually sees the person in the flesh, until he appears
and disclaims having been in that vicinity before.
Sometimes a person usually normal sees a friend
enter a distant building at a certain hour of the
day, which he times, and later verifies from the
friend that he actually entered the building about
that hour. Sometimes an acquaintance is seen talking to a stranger, at a place beyond the normal
powers to discern, and later upon describing the
place and the stranger, the acquaintance verifies the
description as accurate. Happenings seen in dreams,
also, not infrequently are found to be records of
what has actually transpired, or what actually later
comes to pass.

Recorded cases of this kind are so numerous that
a book might easily be filled with them. They reveal that the astral body has sense organs by which
it may recognize that which is happening at a distance. In the case of accident, or the death of an
acquaintance, it is highly probable that there is a

1. Many authentic cases of monitions are given in Thirty Years of Psychical
Research, by Richet, Ch. VI; and in At the Moment of Death, by Flammarion,
Ch. VI.
2. For authentic cases see Death and Its Mystery, by Flammarion, Ch. IX.

conscious or subconscious desire on the part of the person dying or hurt to communicate this information. The wave motions thus sent out are intercepted by the person receiving the information. In other cases it seems that the clairvoyant faculty, or other astral sense organ, has perceived the happening or condition and made the astral brain aware of it. Conditions then have been favorable for the astral brain to impress this information on the physical brain and obtain a conscious recognition of it.

Because of the difficulty experienced by the astral brain in impressing information perceived by it upon physical consciousness, it often makes use of symbols. Because of the association of thoughts, one thought, or image, suggesting another, the astral brain often finds much less resistance to presenting information in symbolic form than to presenting it as conversation or as an image of the happening. It is sometimes easier for it, for instance, to produce the sensation of smelling a strong pipe, to acquaint a person of the astral presence of someone who before death smoked a strong pipe, than to show a phantasm of the person, or to cause his voice to be heard. Symbolism is the easiest method, and the most common one, by which the astral brain transmits information to the everyday consciousness.

But whether it makes use of symbolism, or some more direct method of apprising the external consciousness of something, it is frequently not able to gain the recognition of the external consciousness at the time the information is first perceived. It may be hours, days, or even weeks, after the astral brain recognizes some important fact, before it finds suitable conditions—such as unusually sound sleep, or sufficient lack of alertness to facilitate some involuntary movement—for transmitting the knowledge to the physical brain.

Not all monitions, and not all premonitions are confined to subjective phenomena. Sometimes several persons present see the same vision, or hear the same knock or disturbance, and sometimes physical objects are moved with no one touching them.[3] In such cases either an astral entity, or the astral brain of some person present, uses the electromagnetic emanations of those present to cause a movement of physical matter. Electromagnetic energy derived from organic substance, and preferably from a living person of mediumistic temperament, so far as is now known, is an absolute requisite for the psychic production of movement without physical contact.

In all cases the controlling entity, whether it be the astral brain of some person in the flesh, or some discarnate entity, or merely a strong thought-form, does not generate the energy used. By establishing proper rapport with a source of energy it merely directs it into a given channel. It acts on much the same principle as the electrician who closes a switch that permits an electric current to flow through and set in motion ponderous machinery. The electrician need not be strong to do this, neither need the controlling entity be strong to produce startling phys-

3. For authentic cases see Death and Its Mystery, by Flammarion, Ch. IX.

ical manifestations of psychic phenomena. The entity needs a sufficient supply of electromagnetic energy that has been generated through organic processes, and needs to effect a rapport with the astral substance associated with it. The electromagnetic energy is directed by means of the astral substance associated with it, and when rapport has been established this astral substance may be controlled, if no opposing intelligence is also in rapport with it, with very little effort and in a surprisingly effective manner.

Bilocation.— Similar principles are involved in cases of bilocation. Bilocation takes place when a person appears simultaneously in two different locations. The lives of the saints, and other legendary literature, abound with mention of such cases. Authentic cases are also known at the present day.[4] The double, which appears at a distant spot and perhaps to several persons, and sometimes even moves objects, may be the astral body, or it may be a thought-form.

A thought is primarily certain rates of motion in astral substance that assume a form. Such an astral thought-form may, or may not, be vitalized with electromagnetic energy. That thoughts are capable of communicating such motions is demonstrated through the photography of thought-forms by Dr. Baraduc of France and others. If one person thinks strongly of another, the image of the thinker will be conveyed through astral vibrations to the astral brain of the person thought of. If the person

4. Thirty Years of Psychical Research, by Richet, p. 556; and Death and Its Mystery, by Flammarion, p. 125.

thought of is receptive, his astral brain will perceive this image of the thinker, and if he is accustomed to bring up into everyday consciousness the things he perceives in the astral—if he is sensitive—these rates of motion will be communicated to his physical brain and he will apparently see the person doing the thinking.

Another person, who is not a sensitive, may be present and perceive nothing. But if the thinker has the ability to impart strong electromagnetic motion to the thought-form it is possible to set up such electromagnetic oscillations that it will register as a transparent image upon the physical organs of sight of those who are not in the least psychic. The person may thus be seen distinctly by many people at a long distance from his body. But really he does not leave the physical, only projects a thought-form vitalized with electromagnetic force. By this means he may appear simultaneously in several localities at the same time.

Astral travel.—Yet only a portion of the cases of bilocation can be explained as thought-forms. In other cases, undoubtedly, the person is traveling in his astral body. The electromagnetic emanations of a person may be sent to a distance, or may be used by the astral body to build up a visible form at a long distance from the physical body, but the etheric body, being continuously dependent upon the life processes of the physical, never leaves the close proximity of the physical form. The astral body, however, is not so restricted, and during physical life may almost entirely leave the physical body.

When so absent it is connected with the physical by a very thin line of force in astral substance.

The astral body when absent from the physical may visit the homes of the dead in astral realms, may attend schools on either plane and bring back the memory of what has been seen and heard, or may visit distant physical or astral lands. Full instructions for developing the ability to do these things are presented in the MS., "How to Travel in the Astral," which is given without charge to all members of The Church of Light who pass the final examinations on eleven courses of study. This astral body, being occupied by the mind, or soul, when it appears at a distant place is able to carry on intelligent conversation, which a thought-form can not do. The physical body, meantime, acts in a purely mechanical and automatic manner. In order to become visible to the physical sense of sight, or to move physical objects, the astral body utilizes the electromagnetic emanations of its own physical body, or the electromagnetic emanations of the persons to whom it appears, or who are in the vicinity of the objects moved.

It should be understood that these electromagnetic energies used by astral entities both in the flesh and out of the flesh to produce physical phenomena, are generated by organic life. They are emanations from the etheric counterpart. This etheric counterpart never leaves the physical replica. It is sometimes taught that an etheric "shell" may be drawn from the dead physical body and used to simulate the deceased person. I believe such teaching to be an error, and a close study of the biological processes that generate and maintain the etheric bodies of organic life leads me to conclude that the etheric body is so closely associated with, and dependent upon, the chemical processes of the physical that it never leaves its immediate vicinity.

At death the astral body of man usually severs its connection with the etheric body. The etheric body then has no more intelligence than the physical corpse. It is, in fact, the vitality of the physical body. After death there is still some energy radiated by the corpse until it dissolves, but as the physical body disintegrates so does the etheric body. It might furnish some energy to an astral entity if a point of contact could be established, but not nearly so potent as may be derived from a living person. Its organization is possible only so long as the cells of the body carry on their life processes, for from them it draws its energy. Until the body disintegrates it may hover over the corpse, and is often seen as a phosphorescent light. But I have every reason to believe that it cannot be disconnected from the corpse and used as a vehicle for magical work, or control a medium for the purpose of impersonation.

Etherealization.—In a seance room, and sometimes elsewhere, an astral entity—which may be either a deceased person or one yet in the flesh or a non-human intelligence—by getting in rapport with a medium's astral body may be able to utilize the electromagnetic energy present to rarefy the atmosphere in limited areas and set the atmospheric particles in such rapid vibration as to produce a luminous effect. This luminous area may take the form of a hand or face, or even a human figure. Such a manifestation is called an etherealization.

Or the entity may set the ether to vibrating in a certain spot with the frequency of light. This light may then be moved about the room. Such lights are not infrequent at spirit seances, and are sometimes also seen elsewhere.

Spirit Photographs.— From etherealization to spirit photographs is but a step. If there is a figure present luminous enough to be seen, it probably also can impress a photographic negative. In point of fact, faces of the deceased, messages written in their own handwriting and signed with their signatures, and relating things that only they could know, appear on photographic negatives even when they are invisible to the human eye. Some astral entity has succeeded in utilizing the electromagnetic emanations of those present to set up rates of motion in the ether that impress the negative much as light would do. A photographic negative is much more sensitive to certain high light vibrations than the human eye. So while it is not uncommon for the presence photographed to be seen by persons in the same room, yet it may also be photographed while invisible to the human eye.[5]

Other than human astral entities may likewise be photographed. There are myriads of magnetic elementals, nature spirits, and such creatures, so dense

5. For authentic examples of spirit photography see The Case for Spirit Photography, by A. Conan Doyle.

in their structure and so close to the earth that it takes only a moderate development of clairvoyance to see them. Fairies, pixies, and the like are not mere fables. Their power, no doubt, has often been exaggerated; for it is doubtful if they are able in any manner to affect human life and destiny except through rapport with, and at least partial control of, some human medium. Nevertheless, they exist as astral entities. As such, through rapport with a human medium, they may collect about themselves sufficient of the electromagnetic emanations of the medium to become visible to physical eyes, and to impress a photographic negative with their pictures.[6]

Inspirational speaking.— Another phase of mediumship, one of the most common in fact, is inspirational speaking. A medium takes the rostrum and goes fully or partially under control. Some astral entity may direct the speech that follows, but far more frequently the astral brain of the medium simply receives the thought emanations from the astral brains of the audience. These thoughts—which are not only the conscious opinions of the audience, but also the information contained in their astral brains —are constantly radiating their energy through the astral substance. They are received by the medium's brain and become the source of his inspiration. He gives back to the audience their ideas and opinions colored by his own.

Test readings.—In test readings also, although the medium may have a wider source of informa-

----

6. For authentic photographs of faries see The Coming of the Faries, by A. Conan Doyle.

tion, it is common for the information to be gathered from the minds of the clients. The medium, of course, knows nothing about the source of information. Yet when a question is asked or written, whatever information about the subject is present in the astral brain of the client is radiating energy through astral substance. The medium then tunes in, unconsciously, on these wave motions and combines the various factors so received in a manner that will give a plausible answer.

Trumpet speaking.—Trumpet speaking is still another rather common form of mediumship. The controlling astral entity in such manifestations utilizes the electromagnetic force present to produce motions in the atmosphere within a trumpet or megaphone that give a rate of vibration similar to that used in speaking. These compressions and rarefactions produce the same effect as some one talking. The trumpet is often picked up by invisible hands and carried about the room, talking, singing songs, and laughing. It is probable that the astral vocal chords of the medium, or of the entity, are actually placed in relation to the trumpet just as they would be in speaking through it physically. About these astral vocal chords are attracted compressed air or other atomic matter of sufficient consistency to be used to produce the effect of a physical voice speaking through the trumpet.

Apports.— The carrying of physical objects long distances through no physical agency is a more rare

7. For authentic instances of objects carried without physical contact see Haunted Houses, by Flammarion, Ch. IX.

phase of mediumship.   Objects obtained in this manner are called apports.[7]

The most astounding phenomena in connection with such apports that have come to my attention were those produced some years ago at seances held in Australia under the leadership of the late Mr. Stanford.

The medium was stripped and searched and taken into a room specially prepared by the investigators with the view of making deception impossible.   Under such conditions antiques and other objects of considerable volume and weight, upon demand, suddenly appeared in the midst of the investigators, apparently being pilfered from countries sometimes thousands of miles distant.

To produce such an effect it is necessary not only that the astral body of the medium be able to travel to the spot where the apport is located, but also that he organize lines of electromagnetic force from his physical body to his distant astral body.   This electromagnetic energy, then, must be used as a magnetic force to polarize the protons and electrons within the atoms of the object to be transported. The object when thus reduced to its electronic state may be moved with the speed of electricity along the lines of electromagnetic force established by the medium.   In this dematerialized state physical things would offer no resistance, no more so at least than to radio waves, and the object could be transported into a locked room as easily as anywhere else.   Then when it had reached its destination, if the polarizing force were removed the object would resume its normal shape and properties.

Many years ago Zollner, professor of physical astronomy at Leipzig, experimenting with the medium, Slade, had proof of the movement of objects without contact, and also that matter could be made to pass through matter. This was set forth in his book, Transcendental Physics, now unfortunately out of print. At the present time, since it is known that the electrons of what appears to be solid matter are relatively as far apart as the planets of the solor system—there being about as much space for the particles to pass as there is in proportion to their size for the planets to pass each other—the mystery of matter passing through matter is not so great. If the force used to suspend the motion of the electrons were similer to an electric force, the electrons would not retain their original relative positions, and the form would be completely destroyed. But if the movement of the electrons can be suspended, say, by something similar to a magnetic force, then when matter has passed through matter and the magnetic force is removed, they again resume their original motions, and there appears the original object.

Materialized flowers.— It is difficult to say just what percentage of the flowers that so often suddenly appear, apparently out of space, in a seance room, are really apports and what percentage are materialized flowers. Probably the most of them have been culled from someone's garden and brought to the room by invisible agencies as apports.

On the other hand, it is not impossible that flowers are at times actually materialized. This is not more wonderful than that the materialized form of Katie

King should give Crookes a lock of her hair, or
that the materialization Phygia should permit
Richet to cut hair from her head, or that Mme.
d'Esperance should allow sitters to cut off pieces of
the materialized draperies surrounding her.[8]

Perhaps I may here be pardoned for relating a
personal experience: Many years ago some persons of my acquaintance held regular private
seances at which they sometimes beheld wonderful
phenomena. At one of these circles a person present
wished a token from a loved one long dead. Slate
writing was a common thing in the circle and slates
were present. The controlling entity told the lady
making the request to take off her wedding ring
and lay it on the slate. This was done, and the slate
kept in full sight, although given no special notice
as some of those present were engaged in conversation. Presently, on taking up the slate, the lady
found a beautiful golden rose painted on it. This
rose, which expert jewelers pronounced gold plat-
ing, was as perfect twenty-five years later as on the
day it was painted.

The discarnate person was very fond of roses.
Evidently the electromagnetic forces of the medium
were directed by some astral intelligence in such a
manner as to overcome the cohesion of some of the
atoms of the gold ring and place them in the desired
arrangement to form a rose. It was a case of precipitation in which gold was the substance used.

Materialization.— This brings us to the most wonderful of all psychic phenomena—to materialization.

---

8. Thirty Years of Psychical Research, by Richet, p. 476.

The evidence for the genuineness of materializations is voluminous and quite irrefutable. As a rule they do not form instantly, but gradually condense from a white nebulous vapor about a nucleus. This white vapor, called "ectoplasm", from two words meaning "outside", and "form", is a condensation of the emanations from the medium's body. It is really an extension of the medium's astral body about which physical particles are collected in such a manner as to give it temporarily, and sometimes permanently, the properties of physical substance.

The startling thing about ectoplasm is that it seems capable of assuming the form, shape, and properties, not only of any conceivable inorganic substance, but also of any conceivable living org·· or organism.

Quoting from "Thirty Years of Psychical Research", by Richet:

"In any case we can, thanks to the experiments of Crawford, Ochorowicz, Mme. Bisson, and Schrenck-Notzing, form some idea of the genesis of these phenomena, and sketch out a kind of embryology. This embryo-genesis may not be identical in all cases, but in some that have been exactly observed and illustrated by photography, a kind of nebulous, gelatinous substance exudes from the medium's body and gradually is organized into a living, moving form. The ectoplasmic cloud would seem to become living substance while at the same time veils develop around it that conceal the mechanism of its condensation into living tissues" (page 491).

"I have also, like Geley, Schrenck-Notzing, and

Mme. Bisson, been able to see the first lineaments of materializations as they were formed. A kind of liquid or pasty jelly emerges from the mouth or the breast of Marthe which organizes itself under degrees, acquiring the shape of a face or a limb. Under very good conditions of visibility, I have seen this paste spread on my knee, and slowly take form so as to show the rudiment of the radius, the cubitus, or metacarpal bone whose increasing pressure I could feel on my knee" (page 467.)

In the experiments of Sir Wm. Crookes with the medium Home, everything witnessed took place in the light, and materializations were frequent. His experiments with the medium Florence Cook and the materialization which called itself Katie King were even more conclusive. His letter of March, 1874, says:

"I have at last obtained the absolute proof I have been seeking. On March the 2nd, during a seance at my house, Katie (the apparition), having moved among us, retired behind the curtain and a moment later called me, saying, 'Come into the cabinet and raise my medium's head.' Katie stood before me in her usual white robe and wearing her turban. I went toward the bookcase to raise Miss Cook, and Katie moved aside to let me pass. Miss Cook had slipped down, and I had the satisfaction of seeing that she was not dressed like Katie, but was wearing her usual dress of black velvet."

Crookes says further:

"Katie is six inches taller than Miss Cook; yesterday with bare feet, she was four and one-half inches taller. Her neck was bare and did not show the cicatrice that is on Miss Cooke's neck. Her ears are not pierced, her complexion is very fair, and her fingers much longer than those of Miss Cook."

Richet, speaking of a seance he held with Eusapia Palidino, at which Mme. Curie was present, says:

"It seems hard to imagine a more convincing experiment, for in twenty-nine seconds the element of surprise is eliminated. In this case there was not only the materialization of a hand, but also of a ring. As all experiments demonstrate, materializations of objects, garments, and woven stuffs are simultaneous with human forms, these latter never appearing naked, but covered by veils which are at first white semi-luminous clouds which end by taking the consistence of real woven fabrics."[9]

Many scientific men of international reputation have experimented with numerous materializing mediums and found them genuine, as did Geley who, "after describing very precisely the variations in the gelatinous embryo-plastic mass, adds: 'I do not say merely, There was no trickery, I say, There was no possibility of trickery. Nearly all the materializations took place under my own eyes, and I have observed the whole of their genesis and development.' "[10]

Baron Von Schrenck-Notzing in his book, "Phenomena of Materialization", gives a critical account of his own very extensive experiments, and illustrates it with reproductions from 225 photo-

---

9. Thirty Years of Psychical Research, by Richet, p. 497.
10. Thirty Years of Psychical Research, by Richet, p. 525.

graphs of materialized forms in all their various stages of development as they exude from the medium and take human shape.

Although no further evidence is necessary to make certain the fact that materializations actually take place, still more recent experiments leave no possible loophole of uncertainty. I quote from Richet:

Plaster casts of materializations.—"Geley and I took the precaution of introducing, unknown to any other person, a small quantity of cholesterin in the bath of melted paraffin wax placed before the medium during the seance. This substance is soluble in paraffin without discoloring it, but on adding sulphuric acid it takes a deep violet-red tint; so that we could be absolutely certain that any moulds obtained should be from the paraffin provided by ourselves. We therefore had certain proof that the moulds obtained could not have been prepared in advance but must have been produced during the seance itself. Absolute certainty was thus secured.

"During the seance the medium's hands were held firmly by Geley and myself on the right hand, and on the left, so that he could not liberate either hand. A first mould was obtained of a child's hand, then a second of both hands, right and left; a third time of a child's foot. The creases in the skin and the veins were visible on the plaster casts made from the moulds.

"By reason of the narrowness at the wrist these moulds could not be obtained from living hands, for the whole hand would have to be withdrawn through the narrow opening at the wrist. Professional modellers secure their results by threads attached to the hands, which are pulled through the plaster. In the moulds here considered there was nothing of the sort; they were produced by a materialization followed by a dematerialization, for this latter was necessary to disengage the hand from the paraffin 'glove'.

"These experiments, which we intend to resume on account of their importance, afford an absolute proof of a materialization followed by a dematerialization, for even if the medium had the means to produce the result by a normal process, he could not have made use of them. We defy the most skillful modellers to obtain such moulds, without using the plan of two segments separated by a thread and afterwards united.

"We therefore affirm that there was a materialization and a dematerialization of an ectoplasmic or fluidic hand, and we think that this is the first time that such rigorous conditions of experiment have been imposed."

I may add that the experiments were continued, and casts of folded hands were obtained. Reproductions from photographs of some of these casts are given in the "Scientific American", for November, 1923.

It remains but to be said, in regard to the nature of the materializations, that once formed there is a circulation of the blood, warmth, perspiration, and the other functions exhibited by ordinary flesh and blood, as well as intelligent action. Small pieces of skin left behind when a form dematerialized has been found under the microscope to differ not in the least from ordinary human cuticle. A full formed materialization is actual human flesh and blood as long as it lasts.

In regard to the method by which materialization is accomplished, I believe in all cases the form condenses about a projection of the medium's astral body. The atmosphere contains all the elements of which the body is composed in minute states of subdivision. Such particles, no doubt, may be utilized to assist in building up the materializing form. But recent experiments go to show that in some instances, at least, the material is drawn from the medium's body. Mediums have been weighed before a materialization has taken place, and then again while there was a materialized form present. A comparison of the weights indicates that substance is subtracted from the medium's body. The materialized form, in such instances, approximates in weight the amount lost by the medium. Further, in some instances weighing shows that others present at the seance also lose weight during the manifestation, indicating that they likewise furnish substance for the materializing form.

It appears, then, in those cases in which the materialization is quite bulky, that commonly flesh and blood from those present, chiefly from the medium, is dematerialized, and then gradually materialized about an extension of the medium's astral body. This projection of the medium's astral body may assume any shape, and the materialization will conform to it in contour and texture. When dematerialization takes place the flesh and blood extracted from those present is returned to the original owners.

Not only at seances, but also where there are hauntings, a peculiar cool draught, a draught that gives the impression of rapid evaporation rather than of moving air, is commonly felt just before there are physical manifestations. Such a draught is really the sensation felt when electromagnetic energy is drawn from the person to supply it for the manifestation. In the case of materializations this electromagnetic energy is used to dematerialize physical substance and with it build up a different form. So far as investigations have gone it would seem that all materializations are composed of substance that has not been created at the moment, but that has been drawn from some other already existing matter.

When a complete personality materializes, the astral body of the medium is almost wholly absent and occupying the materialized form. Even as when a person travels in the astral body, only a slight line of communication may connect the astral form and the physical body. Should this line be severed, death ensues. Therefore, it is quite dangerous to the medium unexpectedly to grab a materialized form, and quite dangerous to a person out of the physical body in sleep rudely to awaken him. In either case the shock if severe enough may sever the astral thread connecting the two bodies, or at least cause severe injury to the nervous system.

Hauntings.— A different order of phenomena from any so far considered are hauntings.[11] Hauntings, while of numerous kinds, may roughly be classified in four categories. There are hauntings that only occur in association with some particular person or some particular type of person. There are other hauntings which are not associated with some person or particular type of person, but are associated with some particular locality. Both these phases of hauntings sometimes are obviously associated in some manner with a person who has died or been killed. Both phases, likewise, sometimes occur under such circumstances as to show no association with a dead person, and, indeed, to make such association extremely unlikely.

Localities that are haunted independent of the presence of a person of mediumistic temperament, and which indicate the influence of a dead person, usually are places where death has taken place under great stress of mind. More rarely the place haunted is a locality where the deceased long resided previous to death.

The intense emotion, or mental attitude, chains the astral body to the particular spot, which has become permeated with the electromagnetic emanations of the person during life. These electromagnetic emanations, with which rapport has never been completely severed, enable the entity to exercise considerable physical force. Doors may be opened, physical objects moved, or some tragic event may

---

11. For numerous authentic cases of hauntings see Haunted Houses, by Flammarion.

be performed in pantomime.   When a person goes to sleep after working unusually hard at some routine employment he often repeats the work over and over again in his dreams.   A ghost, such as I have mentioned, because something has been impressed strongly on his emotions, for a very similar reason repeats some act over and over again.   He has not freed himself from a strain to his mentality.   He is said to be earthbound.

Other ghosts appear only in the presence of persons of mediumistic temperament upon whose electromagnetic emanations they draw for force enough to make their presence known.   They, likewise, may be earthbound human beings, not yet freed from some intense emotion.   They may be attached to the locality of death, to the place where they resided before death, or occasionally can manifest themselves at other places through being able to use the electromagnetic emanations of a person to whom they are attached.

As a rule a ghost possesses almost no intelligence, because it is wholly under the control of and dominated by the idea that binds it to earth.   It is like a hypnotized person who has been put to sleep and told to do some one thing over and over.   The hypnotic subject does this, and pays no attention to anything else, being quite oblivious to the presence and questions of others.   Ghosts of this class are deceased human beings under the influence of powerful auto-suggestion.

If they can be induced to talk they may be convinced of the error of their ways and go about their business in the astral world and cease to burden the earth with their presence. But it is like trying to argue with a subject in the deep hypnotic state. Usually they can perceive only the idea that dominates them. If the idea is to perform some physical task, such as returning stolen money or giving some information, as soon as this is accomplished they haunt no more and pass into other regions on the astral plane.

Differing from the above in that they show no association with a person who has died are the so-called poltergeist phenomena.

Noises, uproars, the throwing of sticks and stones by unseen hands, the opening and closing of doors by invisible agency, the movement of furniture and breaking of crockery without physical contact, and other phenomena of a trivial or mischievous character are rather more numerous than most people suppose. This class of phenomena is usually due to non-human astral entities called elementals.

In far the more numerous cases of this kind the phenomena take place only in the presence of a certain person, who is often an adolescent boy or girl.

Mischievous astral entities are able to get in rapport with such persons of unusual mediumistic tendencies and use their electromagnetic emanations to manifest physical violence. In some instances it is also quite possible that the astral counterpart of the mediumistic individual has a part in directing the phenomena. When the mediumistic individual departs from the vicinity, in these cases, either the phenomena follow the medium, or cease.

In still more rare instances these poltergeist phenomena take place in certain localities irrespective of how many persons are present, and irrespective of any person being in the immediate vicinity. If people take notice of the phenomena, or of a human ghost, electromagnetic energy sometimes is drawn from them to strengthen the manifestation, their thoughts establishing a line of communication for the transfer of energy. Such phenomena are made possible through the electromagnetic emanations of people's thoughts being made use of by elementals. These thought-forms may converge at certain places due to a variety of causes. A building so haunted, or one haunted by a human ghost, when torn down usually destroys the condition of rapport, and there being no adequate supply of electromagnetic energy to draw upon, the phenomena cease.

Fake mediums.—Let us now return to the subject of mediums.

It should be understood that a demonstration of mediumistic power requires the expenditure of energy. The medium himself radiates a limited supply of electromagnetic energy, and the other persons present also a limited amount. Enough energy is only occasionally available to make a thrilling demonstration. But the public, ignoring this fact, demands that the medium repeat the phenomena every time he is asked. This is just as sensible as to ask an athlete who has established a world record as a foot racer to repeat his best work on all occasions.

Certain conditions are necessary for the athlete to establish a record, and certain conditions are necessary for a medium to do his best work. If, because a medium cannot under different circumstances and at different times repeat his performance, we assert his claims are false, we also should demand that a world champion runner be able to make his record again any time we suggest, without going into training, without spiked shoes, and on the pavement or in the mud. As a matter of fact, an athlete is seldom able to reach his record more than once. Likewise, if a medium once produces genuine phenomena, about which there can be no doubt because all possibility of trickery has been guarded against, this establishes the phenomena as real.

It has been objected by some that the condition of darkness imposed at some seances is merely to facilitate fraud. Yet the same criticism might be leveled at radio operators. Radio messages do not carry so well in sunlight as in darkness, and strange to say some radio operators claim that moonlight is beneficial to radio work. They say that a message will carry farther from east to west when the full moon has just risen than at any other time. Yet why admit that a noon day sun interferes with radio and not admit that it may interfere with psychic phenomena?

It is related of the famed discoverer of photography that in order to bring his invention before the public he desired to take a photograph of a famous court beauty. He diligently explained the condition that was necessary: that he could only take the picture by sunlight. As the lady knew she appeared to better advantage by the false light of the evening ball-room, she insisted her picture be taken by lamp-light. As the inventor could not take the photograph as demanded, he was laughed out of court, and his discovery called a hoax. All the evidence goes to show that it takes more energy to produce physical manifestations of psychic phenomena in the light than it does in the dark.

To be sure, it is probable that any good medium will perpetrate frauds under given circumstances. We might almost say that in negative mediumship unless the medium is sufficiently under control to be quite unaware of what he is doing the results are not of the best.

A hypnotized subject tries to do whatever he is told, and even though he is going through a lot of nonsense, believes he is performing as he is told to do. If he is told to smoke a cigar, and no cigar is at hand, he will proceed to smoke a stick, and if he has no match, goes through the motion of lighting one, and is unconscious of the fact that he is not strictly carrying out his orders.

Of course there is no excuse for mediums who premeditate fraud. But once a medium is in the trance state he is no more responsible for his actions than is a hypnotized subject. If those present demand a certain type of phenomena, this suggestion takes hold of the mind, and he tries to produce them. He may be able to produce genuine phenomena, just as the hypnotized subject would actually smoke a cigar if one were present. But if genuine phenomena are not forthcoming, the suggestion to produce them has the effect of causing him to stimulate them to the best of his ability. For this he is nowise responsible, for one of the essential conditions of this kind of mediumship is that the medium must be unconscious of and irresponsible for his actions while under control. If fraud takes place, which is not prepared for in advance by the medium, the only ones at fault are the experimenters, whose duty it is to make fraud impossible.

Even in clairaudience, clairvoyance, psychometry, telepathy, and prevision, the irresponsible medium only hears, sees, feels, thinks, or has cognizance of, what is imparted to him by his control. Everything is second hand, and depends for its veracity upon both the integrity and the ability of the controlling entity. On the other hand, the person who develops these faculties by the integrative method is not dependent upon another for information. He uses his astral sense organs as he does his physical sense organs. He controls himself and his faculties. This is the difference between disintegrative mediumship and mastership.

CPSIA information can be obtained at www.ICGtesting.com
Printed in the USA
BVOW03s1451080414

350076BV00021B/1340/P